25
BICYCLE TOURS
on Delmarva

25
BICYCLE TOURS
on Delmarva

Cycling the Chesapeake Bay Country

John R. Wennersten

with the assistance of Stewart M. Wennersten

SECOND EDITION

Backcountry Publications
Woodstock · Vermont

An invitation to the reader

Although it is unlikely that the roads you cycle on these tours will change much with time, some road signs, landmarks, and other items may. If you find that changes have occurred on these routes, please let us know so we may correct them in future editions. The author and publisher also welcome other comments and suggestions. Address all correspondence to:

Editor, 25 Bicycle Tours ™ Series
Backcountry Guides
PO Box 748
Woodstock, Vermont 05091

Library of Congress Cataloging-in-Publication Data

Wennersten, John R.

    25 bicycle tours on Delmarva : cycling the Chesapeake Bay country / John R. Wennersten with the assistance of Stewart M. Wennersten. — 2nd ed.

    p. cm.

ISBN 0-88150-338-X

    1. Bicycle touring—Delmarva Peninsula—Guidebooks. 2. Delmarva Peninsula—Guidebooks. I. Wennersten, Stewart M. II. Title.

GV1045.5.D45W46   1995

917.52'1—dc20

95-9998

CIP

10 9 8 7 6 5

Printed in the United States of America

Text and cover design by Sally Sherman
Cover photograph by G & J Images/ The Image Bank
Maps by Richard Widhu, © 1988, 1995 Backcountry Publications

Published by Backcountry Guides,
a division of The Countryman Press, Inc.,
PO Box 748, Woodstock, Vermont 05091.

Acknowledgments

This book has its origins in a series of Sunday afternoon bicycle rides in Wicomico and Somerset Counties on Maryland's Eastern Shore. Often I rode with my sons Matthew and Stewart. They were of indefatigable good humor and possessed reservoirs of strength that bolstered my spirits on long, hard trips. In many respects this book was a family enterprise, and my sons, my wife, and I had good times together while we rediscovered the Chesapeake Bay country on bicycle. On many trips I was also accompanied by my friends Nat Stelzner and Dave Cowall. Later, as the book took form, I recruited other friends into taking the tours with me.

I am especially indebted to Richard Keenan for accompanying me on century tours, one of which was made in cold, wet weather. Trucks passed, drenching us in their spray. Yet we plodded on. Ours was the buoyant enthusiasm that comes only from inexperience.

Since this book was first published, I have received a large number of encouraging letters and telephone calls from cyclists who have used this touring guide. Their insights and helpful remarks have made the task of revising this book more pleasant than it might otherwise have been.

I owe special thanks to Don Cathcart, a marathon runner, who helped me stay in decent middle-aged condition over hard winter months, and to George Demko, who experienced the joys of the Dorchester marsh and who over countless chats learned more about cycling on the Delmarva Peninsula than he wanted to know.

During the preparation of this book I rode a Bridgestone 500 bicycle. In the course of logging about 3500 miles on the highways of the Delmarva Peninsula, I learned a lot about bikes and a lot about strength and endurance. I once thought I would be the last person to write a book on bicycling. It's been one of those happy convergences of man, geography, and bike.

Lastly, Ruth Ellen, my wife, put up with my bicycle obsession. She alone knows the value of the 26th tour.

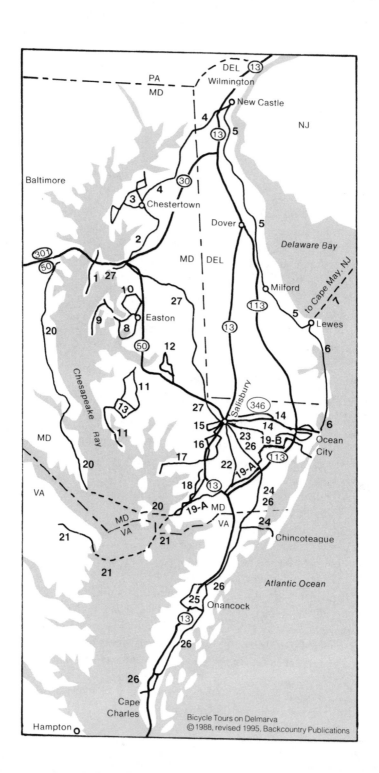

Contents

TWO CHESAPEAKE CENTURIES 197

Preface to the Second Edition

When I wrote this book in 1988 I did so with a small but dedicated audience of recreational cyclists in mind. Little did I know how successful it would be or how wide an audience it would find. Since the first printing of this book, a revolution in cycling has occurred in Chesapeake Bay country. Each year now thousands of cyclists pedal the quiet country lanes and visit the sedate towns and villages that dot the Chesapeake countryside. Bike clubs and professional touring groups schedule trips on the Delmarva Peninsula. Cyclists have become familiar figures on the Chesapeake landscape. The land is flat and visually attractive. Accommodations are abundant, and there are many cultural activities.

I have received so many inquiries from readers about bed & breakfast accommodations along cycle routes that I have expanded this section of the book. After a hard day on a bicycle, riders demand a comfortable, enjoyable evening and rest. I have also included more material on museums and tourist attractions in Chesapeake Bay country.

Because this region is subject to heavy tourist pressure in the summer, you may wish to use the Maryland Reservation Service to book hotels, inns, and B&Bs anywhere in Maryland. The service is free. In-state call 410-263-9084; from out of state, call 1-800-654-9303.

The size of the Delmarva Peninsula and its proximity to urban centers allow you to see a lot of it in one or two cycling trips. However, once you get "sand between your toes," I know you'll return again and again to Chesapeake country. The region is made for both lazy town-to-town touring and muscular centuries. So enjoy!

Introduction

The Eastern Shore or Delmarva is a long peninsula lying between the Chesapeake Bay and the Atlantic Ocean. Stretching from Cecil and New Castle Counties in the north, the region follows the Chesapeake Bay south to form a diamond of tidewater counties shaped over the millennia by the sand deposits of the Susquehanna River. Three states—DELaware, MARyland, and VirginiA—have sovereignty on the Eastern Shore, and the name Delmarva (as the region is popularly referred to) testifies to the social allegiance of its inhabitants.

Until recently the Eastern Shore was isolated from the commercial and metropolitan mainstream of Washington, Baltimore, and Wilmington. Lack of good roads in predominantly rural Delaware prevented commercial penetration of the region. The Chesapeake Bay also isolated Maryland's Eastern Shore population until the construction of the William Preston Lane Bridge from Annapolis to Kent Island in 1952. The inhabitants of Virginia's tightly knit Eastern Shore farming communities, with their time-honored ways and local customs, often frustrate the cosmopolitan government of Richmond.

On Delmarva, look to the water. It is a region defined by the Chesapeake Bay and numerous exquisitely beautiful tidal rivers. Its creeks and snug harbors have provided a livelihood for Chesapeake oystermen and fisher folk since the days of Captain John Smith in the 17th century. The region today is a sailor's delight, and cyclists on the Eastern Shore will see watercraft as diverse as giant oil tankers and Chesapeake Bay skipjacks (oyster-dredging sailboats built over 100 years ago).

Most of Delmarva is flat coastal plain, making cycling on the peninsula an easy ride. South of the Choptank River in Maryland, the countryside is as flat as a pancake. The northern part of the Delmarva Peninsula consists of flat stretches interspersed with rolling hills. One obstacle to cyclists on the Eastern Shore is variable winds, especially those out of the south, which can be especially frustrating to the inexperienced cyclist.

Were you to fly over the Delmarva Peninsula in an airplane, you would be struck by the simple fact that the Eastern Shore is the last major green space (over 5000 square miles) between Boston and Richmond. It is a land of loblolly pine and honeysuckle and fields loaded with grain, corn, and truck produce. Delmarva is also the chicken-producing capital of the Atlantic seaboard, and the landscape is dotted with thousands of chicken houses that are part of a billion-dollar industry. Occasionally while biking you will savor the peculiar aroma of these chicken houses. The poultry industry provides a market for local grain producers and thus contributes greatly to agricultural stability in the region.

The marine climate of the Chesapeake Bay and the Atlantic Ocean makes winters mild. (I have cycled in Ocean City in mid-December in 60-degree weather.) Temperatures rarely plunge below the freezing mark, and except during January and February, it is possible to cycle in all seasons on Delmarva. Summers on the Eastern Shore, however, are ferociously hot and humid, almost subtropical in nature. Cyclists who travel Delmarva in July and August are urged to take precautions against heat stroke. Cycle from dawn till about 11 AM in the summer to make the maximum mileage and avoid the hottest hours. The Eastern Shore also receives an inordinately heavy rainfall (some 49 inches per year), and the squalls of summer and autumn can at times be fierce. Wise cyclists would do well to take training rides in the rain and to pack appropriate rain gear made of fabric that wicks away moisture.

Delmarva, one of the earliest settled areas in the United States, has a rich history. Many farm and seafaring families can trace their ancestry back several generations in the same locale. Pride of birth and heritage are an important part of Eastern Shore life, and local residents like to boast that "a hundred years ain't a very long time on the Eastern Shore." The Delmarva Peninsula is an exquisite gem of Americana. Its gristmills, churches, colonial villages, and small towns offer a vision of an America that has all but vanished with the onslaught of metropolitan sprawl surrounding the region.

The Delmarva Peninsula is meant to be savored and explored; it should not be viewed as a physical obstacle to be conquered. The country roads wind leisurely across the rural landscape, and cyclists are largely free from the kind of harassment from motorists that is characteristic of suburbia. "Set a spell," Eastern Shoremen say, inviting you to enjoy the land, its way of life, and its people. Here on Delmarva you can enjoy a crabcake sandwich at a watermen's restaurant in Rock Hall, investigate the colonial architecture of New Castle, or explore the salt-marsh expanses of wild Assateague. The Eastern Shore is a magical land of heritage and beauty. Don't hurry. Set a spell.

Crossing the Chesapeake Bay Bridge

A significant number of cyclists will be approaching the Delmarva Peninsula from Annapolis and the west, using the William Preston Lane Memorial Bridge to cross the Chesapeake Bay. These double spans stride the Chesapeake like behemoths, and although it would be a delight to pedal across to the Eastern Shore, cycling is strictly prohibited.

Bicycles in Maryland are prohibited from expressways, from certain controlled-access highways, and from all toll facilities, like the Chesapeake Bay Bridge. The State Department of Transportation, however, recognizes that this prohibition causes problems for long-distance cyclists, so the Maryland Transportation Authority offers a courtesy transportation service for cyclists. As "time and personnel permit," it will carry cyclists over the bridge in a van at the normal car toll. This service, you should note, is a courtesy and not a matter of standard operating policy. If you wish to cross the William Preston Lane Memorial Bridge from Sandy Point (Annapolis) to Kent Island, please phone in advance of your arrival. Contact bridge authorities at 410-757-6000. Also call ahead when traveling from the opposite direction to make arrangements for a pickup location and time.

Chesapeake Bay Ferry Service

One of the truly glorious aspects of biking on the Delmarva Peninsula is riding ferries across the bay to Tangier and Smith Islands. Both islands have been inhabited since the 17th century, and many of these islanders still speak a vernacular reminiscent of Shakespearean England. So put your bicycle on a boat and go surging across Chesapeake Bay to fishing islands that time has largely forgotten. Also, it is possible to go from Crisfield, Maryland, via Tangier Island, Virginia, to Reedville, Virginia, on the western shore of the Chesapeake. This route is a great way to add to your trip some cycling in historic regions of tidewater Virginia.

Ferry Schedules and Fees

1. *Captain Tyler* (410-425-2771)—Crisfield, Maryland, to Smith Island, Maryland. Operates each day from Memorial Day to September 30. Departs Somers Cove Marina, Crisfield, at 12:30 PM; returns at 5:30 PM. 150-passenger capacity. $17 per person, includes meal. Bicycles travel free with fare.
2. *Captain Jason* (410-425-2351)—Crisfield, Maryland, to Smith Island, Maryland. Operates each day year-round. Departs Crisfield at 12:30 PM and 5 PM. Ferry returns to Crisfield at 8 AM and 4 PM. 150-passenger capacity. $10 round trip. Bicycles permitted.
3. *Island Belle II* mail boat (410-425-4271) (recommended)—Crisfield, Maryland, to Smith Island and Tangier Island, Virginia. Operates year-round. Departs Crisfield at 12:30 PM and 5 PM. Ferry returns at 8 AM and 4:30 PM. 50-passenger capacity. $5 round trip. Bicycles permitted at $2 per bike.
4. *Steven Thomas* (410-968-2338)—Crisfield, Maryland, to Tangier Island, Virginia. Operates May 1 to October 31. Departs Crisfield at 12:30 PM. Ferry returns at 5:15 PM. 316-passenger capacity. $18 round trip; bikes $2 extra.
5. *Captain Evans* (804-453-3430)—Reedville, Virginia, to Smith Island, Maryland. Operates May 1 to October 15. Departs Reedville at 10 AM. Ferry returns at 4 PM. 150-passenger capacity. $10 each way; $2 fee per bicycle.

Attractions

The Delmarva Peninsula has a wealth of historic sites, museums, and outdoor parks. Each trip description will contain information on all the important points of interest. There is scarcely a town or village on the Eastern Shore that does not have a visible presence that reminds the cyclist of the region's rich colonial and 19th-century heritage.

Helpful Hints

Although the Eastern Shore of the Delmarva Peninsula is easy riding, you should be in good biking shape with the ability to cycle as far as your longest planned day trip. The Eastern Shore is especially popular with the "mature" (over age 40) cyclist. The author of this book is 54 years old and has been cycling this region for more than 15 years.

Define your goals for each trip. If you are cycling in a group, make sure everyone agrees on the same goals of mileage, speed, and points of interest.

Reconcile yourself to the fact that you may encounter feisty dogs on your trips. Many otherwise quiet dogs become obnoxious when they spot someone on a bike. You can usually outrun them. If necessary, yell "no!" as loud as you can. This usually stops them long enough for you to speed away. But sometimes wit and speed fail. In the last case I have had great success using a chemical pepper spray called Halt. Halt is sold in most bike shops and causes no lasting harm to dogs.

Carry a bicycle maintenance book and tools for adjusting the brakes and fixing flats. Carry a tire patch kit, extra tubes, a good bike pump, and first-aid materials.

Overestimate the amount of money that you will need. The Eastern Shore is a very popular tourist area, and hotels and motels can be expensive. At the end of each trip I shall identify lodging that I think is a good value for the cyclist.

Avoid the "making distance" syndrome. Stop often, walk away from your bike, bend over and smell the flowers. This activity breaks the monotony of the ride and helps to minimize saddle and hand numbness, the bane of bikers. Eat lightly during breakfast and lunch. When you have finished riding for the day, treat yourself to a hearty evening meal, especially one high in carbohydrates.

A final caution: On weekends during the peak summer season, some highways may have large amounts of tourist automobile traffic. This is especially true for beach areas like Lewes, Delaware, and Ocean City, Maryland. In summer these areas are best explored during weekdays or in the very early morning.

Always wear a helmet! Your head and personal health are worth the investment. I recommend the Bell Tourlite, which is well designed and highly protective. Use a helmet that will provide you with the optimum safety and maximum amount of comfort for hot weather.

Resources

One of the major problems still faced by cyclists, regardless of experience and ability, is locating information on how and where to bike in specific regions. While this book does not pretend to be the final reference text, it does contain some information sources that may prove helpful to you.

Maryland

Bicycle Affairs Coordinator (1-800-252-8776), Maryland Highway Administration, 707 N. Calvert St., Baltimore, MD 21203.

Delaware

Bicycle Coordinator (302-736-3167), Delaware Department of Transportation, PO Box 778, Dover, DE 19903.

Virginia

Bicycle Coordinator (804-786-2964), Virginia Department of Transportation, 1401 E. Broad St., Richmond, VA 23219.

Recommended Books

Tom Cuthbertson, *Anybody's Bike Book,* Ten Speed Press, 1979.

Richard Ballantine, *Richard's Bicycle Book,* Ballantine Press, 1976.

Tom Lieb, *Everybody's Book of Bicycle Riding,* Rodale Press, 1981.

Editors of *Bicycling Magazine, Basic Maintenance and Repair,* Rodale Press, 1990.

John R. Wennersten, *Maryland's Eastern Shore,* Cornell Maritime Press, 1992.

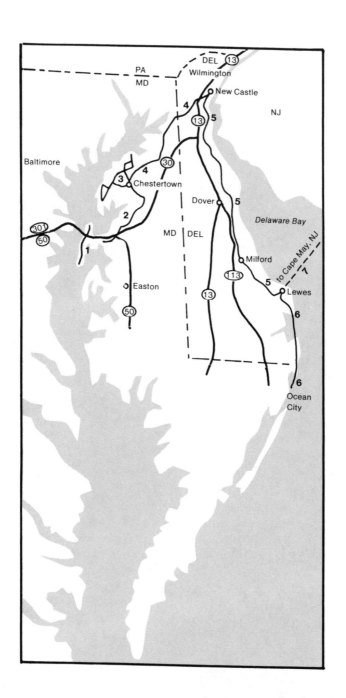

THE UPPER CHESAPEAKE BAY COUNTRY

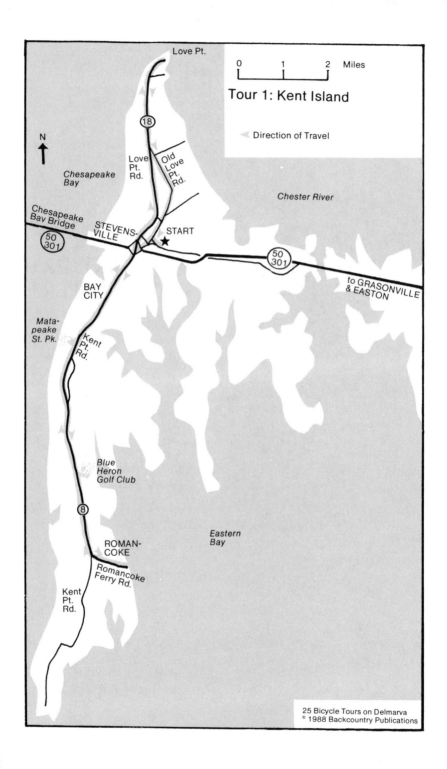

Love Pt.

0   1   2   Miles

Tour 1: Kent Island

◁ Direction of Travel

18

Love
Pt.
Rd.

Old
Love
Pt.
Rd.

*Chesapeake
Bay*

Chester River

*Chesapeake
Bay Bridge*

STEVENS-
VILLE

★ START

50
301

50
301

to GRASONVILLE
& EASTON

BAY
CITY

*Mata-
peake
St. Pk.*

Kent
Pt.
Rd.

*Blue
Heron
Golf Club*

8

ROMAN-
COKE

*Eastern
Bay*

Romancoke
Ferry Rd.

Kent
Pt.
Rd.

25 Bicycle Tours on Delmarva
© 1988 Backcountry Publications

1

Kent Island

Distance: *30 miles*
Terrain: *Flat*
Location: *Queen Anne's County, Maryland*
Special features: *Stevensville, Matapeake State Park, Romancoke, Love Point, views of the Chesapeake Bay Bridge*

Three roads—MD 8, MD 18, and US 50—form a cross of highways on Kent Island. The principal ride of exploration on Kent Island is the north-south route from Love Point to Romancoke.

Kent Island was settled in 1631 when William Claiborne, a Virginia adventurer, placed a trading post on the island. This was 3 years before Lord Baltimore's settlers reached St. Mary's. In the 17th century, Kent Island was an important center of the Chesapeake fur trade with the Susquehannock tribe that lived to the north. It was also an important prize in the territorial squabbles between the Calvert family and the Virginia colony as to land rights and political sovereignty in the region. William Claiborne and the Lords Baltimore fought in court and intrigued politically for three decades over who had the title to and control of Kent Island. The Calverts ultimately prevailed but had to campaign incessantly with lawyers and use the force of arms to win their case.

In the days before the Chesapeake Bay Bridge was constructed, Kent Island was an important auto ferry terminus. Today Kent Island is experiencing phenomenal metropolitan growth, and the sleepy island of small farms and fishing communities is being transformed by suburban development. On the country roads of Kent Island, automobile traffic can be brisk and even dangerous. *The cyclist is advised to use extreme caution on this route.*

Given the geography of Kent Island, it is impossible to make a loop

The Chesapeake Bay Bridge (*photo by Orlando V. Wootten*)

ride. The easiest strategy is to divide the ride into two segments, using Stevensville as a base. After crossing the Chesapeake Bay Bridge, take the first exit to Stevensville. Our ride begins at the parking lot of Stevensville Middle School on MD 18.

Directions for the Ride—Romancoke Segment

0.0 **Stevensville. From the parking lot of the Stevensville Middle School turn left and proceed west on MD 18.**

Despite growth in the area, Stevensville still retains its Victorian charm. Local churches and fire departments sponsor community suppers, and the island community has an active arts league. Many of the 19th-century homes have been restored and are gaily decorated with overflowing flower boxes in summer.

0.6   At the junction of MD 8, proceed cautiously along the US 50 overpass and continue south on MD 8 toward Romancoke.

1.7   Christ Church historical marker commemorates the site of the first Christian congregation in Maryland.

2.3   Bay City, one of several small developments on the island, affords a view of Broad Creek and the Chesapeake Bay Bridge.

3.5   **Matapeake State Park.**

The state of Maryland has transformed the old ferry terminal into a small but lovely fishing, boating, and picnicking area. As you picnic on the shaded grounds of Matapeake, you have a stunning view of the Chesapeake Bay Bridge in the distance. The bridge stands 198.5 feet above the water when it crosses the Chesapeake ship channel and affords ample room for the many freighters that traverse the bay.

6.3   **Queen Anne Marina. Turn right at the Blue Heron Golf Club.**

A small marina and restaurant are located here, and you can take light refreshment and spend time at a favorite Chesapeake hobby—boat watching.

9.2   **Romancoke.**

This town was once the terminus for a ferry from Claiborne in Talbot County. A small park and fishing wharf are here at the old terminal site. Out-of-county residents have to pay a fee if they wish to launch their boats here. On a clear day you can easily see the shoreline of Talbot County to the southeast.

Return to Stevensville on MD 8.

Directions for the Ride—Love Point Segment

0.0   At the junction of MD 18 and MD 8 proceed north on MD 18.

This is one area of Kent Island still dotted with working farms as yet untouched by suburban development.

4.3   **Love Point.**

Now a quiet village, Love Point was until 1952 an important terminus for ferries from Baltimore. The old ferry wharf is privately owned and is not open to the public. Nevertheless, from Love Point at the end of MD 18 you have a fine view of the bay.

6.3 *Returning from Love Point, turn left on Old Love Point Road and follow this road into Stevensville.*

10.5 *Turn left on MD 18 at the Chevron Station. Stevensville Middle School will be on your right.*

Bicycle Repair Services

None on this route.

Attractions

Chesapeake Antique Center (410-827-6640), US 301, Queenstown, MD. Multidealer antiques marketplace, open Saturday and Sunday.

Kent Island Federation of Art (410-643-7424), 405 Main St., Stevensville, MD. Open Friday and Saturday 1–4 PM. Concerts, art showings, and theater.

Lodging

Chesapeake Motel (410-827-7272), US 50 and US 301, Grasonville, MD 21638.

Kent Manor Inn (410-643-5757), 500 Kent Manor Dr., Stevensville, MD 21666. 24 rooms, private baths, moderate rates.

2

Kent Narrows–Chestertown

Distance: *30 miles one way*
Terrain: *Flat to gently rolling*
Location: *Queen Anne's and Kent Counties, Maryland*
Special features: *Kent Narrows, Queenstown, Centreville, Chester River, Chestertown*

This tour is an excellent introduction to the historic towns, villages, and old homes of Maryland's Eastern Shore. You will pass prosperous farms along peaceful country roads that wind lazily north and west through Queen Anne's and Kent Counties. Founded in 1706, Queen Anne's County is named for England's Queen Anne (1665–1714), the last of the Stuart sovereigns, whose short reign of 12 years proved to be one of the most successful in English history. Kent County traces its origins to 1658 when it was named by adventurer and fur trader William Claiborne for the estuary of Kent that adjoined Westmoreland County, England.

The county capital of Queen Anne's is Centreville, and as the name implies, this prosperous little town lies in the center of the county. Proudly perched on the banks of the Chester River, Chestertown is the county seat of Kent, and Chestertown traces its name to the episcopal city of Chester in the English county of Cheshire.

The traffic on the two highways of your journey, MD 18 and MD 213, is pleasantly light. Most tourists follow US 301 for their auto excursions on this part of the Eastern Shore.

The ride starts at Kent Narrows in the shadow of a large drawbridge that connects Kent Island with the Eastern Shore. Some of the finest yachts in the region pass from Eastern Bay in the south through Kent Narrows to the deeper waters of the Chesapeake. To get to Kent Narrows, proceed from the Chesapeake Bay Bridge 2.7 miles to the Kent Narrows

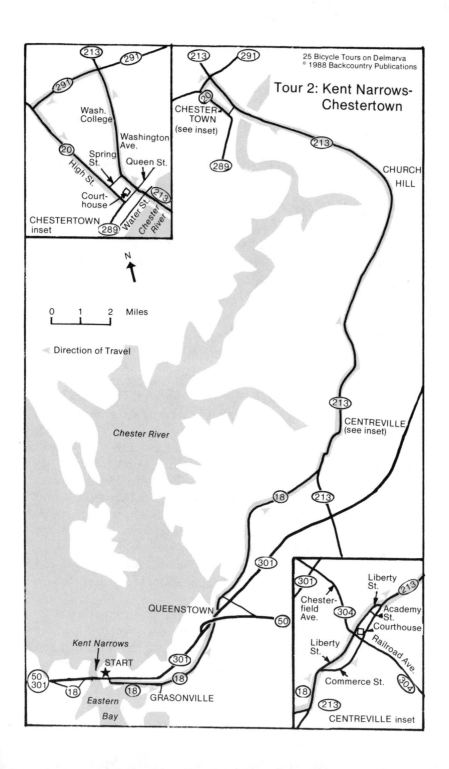

25 Bicycle Tours on Delmarva
© 1988 Backcountry Publications

Tour 2: Kent Narrows-
Chestertown

213   291

213   291

291

213

20

Wash.
College

CHESTER-
TOWN
(see inset)

CHURCH
HILL

Washington
Ave.

213

20

Spring
St.

Queen St.

289

High St.

Court-
house

CHESTERTOWN
inset

289   213

Water St.

Chester
River

N

0   1   2   Miles

Direction of Travel

213

Chester River

CENTREVILLE
(see inset)

18   213

301

301

213

Liberty
St.

QUEENSTOWN

50

Chester-
field
Ave.

304

Academy
St.
Courthouse

Kent Narrows

START

301

18

Liberty
St.

Railroad Ave.

50
301

18

18

304

Eastern
Bay

GRASONVILLE

18

Commerce St.

213

CENTREVILLE inset

drawbridge. At the end of the drawbridge take a sharp right. At the intersection of MD 18 and US 50 turn right and proceed to the Angler Restaurant (the restaurant is at the end of MD 18 at the water's edge). There are several seafood restaurants with ample parking here, and the Angler Restaurant is open in the morning for breakfast.

From the Angler Restaurant you will proceed east on MD 18 through Grasonville. At 5.3 miles you will come to the intersection of MD 18 and US 50. US 50 is the main thoroughfare to the Atlantic beaches in the summer, so use extreme caution when crossing. After crossing US 50, continue on MD 18 to Queenstown and Centreville. At Centreville you will take MD 213, which leads to the Chester River and Chestertown. The ride across the Chester River Bridge is magnificent with views of the yachts in the river and the mansions dotting the opposite shore.

Directions for the Ride

0.0   Angler Restaurant. Proceed east on MD 18.

In summer you can sit at this restaurant's outside tables, have coffee, and watch the great boats pass through Kent Narrows.

0.6   Oyster Cove.

This is one of several expensive condominium communities that have recently sprung up in the Kent Island area.

1.2   Grasonville.

This sleepy town has a few antiques shops and bargain stores. Given its proximity to Annapolis, the town is becoming a commuter suburb.

5.3   Intersection of MD 18 and US 50.

After crossing US 50 you may wish to stop briefly at the Amish Pennsylvania Market. Here the traditional Amish sell a variety of foods brought down from Lancaster, Pennsylvania.

5.6   At the stop sign turn left. Cross US 301 and continue on MD 18 to Queenstown.

6.1   Queenstown.

Originally the county seat of Queen Anne's County, Queenstown has a number of fine homes and the original courthouse built in

1708. Once a thriving port on Queenstown Creek, the town was attacked by the British during the War of 1812. Although tobacco farming and slavery took root here in the 17th century, most farmers in Queen Anne's and Kent had switched to raising wheat and corn by the American Revolution.

6.3 *Just outside Queenstown is the lovely St. Luke's Episcopal Church.*

Rest on its shady lawn and notice the elaborate Star of David in the large church window.

10.0 *Queen Anne's County 4-H Fairgrounds and birthplace marker of Charles Wilson Peale, the famous painter of George Washington.*

12.6 *End of MD 18 and intersection of MD 213. Turn left into Centreville. MD 213 is divided into 2 one-way streets through town.*

13.0 *Centreville. In Centreville, MD 213 becomes Commerce Street.*

This is a well-kept county seat with many fine 18th- and 19th-century homes. A market center for the region, Centreville is the kind of pleasant and well-knit country town that would fit into a Norman Rockwell painting. The Court House on the square was completed in 1792 and is the oldest courthouse in Maryland still in use. In the center of the courthouse square, you will find a statue of Queen Anne. Also of interest are the fine Victorian buildings of Lawyers Row parallel to the Court House.

During the Civil War, Centreville was occupied by Federal troops because of the rebel sympathies of the local population. Judge Richard Carmichael was dragged from his bench and arrested in May 1862, when he attempted to prevent illegal searches and seizures by the Union Army in the town. When he was released from prison 7 months later, he received a hero's welcome and resumed his judicial duties.

13.8 *As you leave Centreville on Commerce Street/MD 213, look for Academy Street on your left.*

The Academy was the old private school for planters' children. Near the Academy at 202 Liberty Street is a picture-perfect brick

Lawyers Row in Centreville, Maryland

house built in 1800 with double chimneys. Also of architectural interest is Wright's Chance, a gambrel-roofed house built in the 1740s, at 119 Commerce Street.

29.0 *Chester River Bridge.*

Like many of the bridges of the Eastern Shore, this one was built by the WPA during the 1930s.

30.0 *Chestertown.*

Founded in 1698, Chestertown is the colonial gem of the Eastern Shore. It boasts many fine period homes, and High and Water Streets retain their charm to this day.

After crossing the bridge into Chestertown, proceed up Washington Avenue to Washington College.

Chartered in 1782, Washington College is the nation's 10th oldest institution of higher learning. Also, it is the only college of that name having had a direct association with George Washington. President Washington was a friend of the college, and his portrait by Rembrandt Peale, the son of Charles Wilson Peale and a famous artist in his own right, is on view in the administration building.

31.2 At the intersection of MD 291 and Washington Avenue bear left on MD 291 and loop over to High Street where you turn left again.

This lovely strand has a number of fine shops with Colonial-style fronts, a town square with a cast-iron fountain, and a famous Lawyers Row adjacent to the Court House.

Proceed down High Street toward the Chester River.

The old Customs House stands on your right at the corner of Front and High Streets and dates from the 1730s. During the colonial period, Chestertown was the center of a rich trade in grain, lumber, and molasses with the Caribbean countries.

Near this site on May 23, 1774, irate citizens boarded the sloop *William Geddes* and threw its load of tea into the Chester River to protest the Intolerable Acts of the British government that had closed the port of Boston. Each year on a weekend in late May, the town hosts a Tea Party Festival that includes fife and drum parades, a reenactment of the *Geddes* tea party, crafts fairs, and garden parties. While tourists are a part of local life, they have not overwhelmed the town, and Chestertown continues to be known for its sophistication and good manners.

A Note for the Return Ride

You can return to Kent Narrows via the same route that you took to Chestertown or you can arrange to be met by car or van in Chestertown. As you may not wish to undertake a 30-mile return by bike, the second choice seems more practical.

Bicycle Repair Services

Bikework (410-778-6940), 208 Cross St., Chestertown, MD.

Attractions

Emmanuel Episcopal Church, Cross St., Chestertown, MD. Built in 1768, this church is known for its Tiffany window.

Tucker House (410-643-8908), 124 S. Commerce St., Centreville, MD. Built in 1794, this museum of Queen Anne's County history is the oldest house in Centreville. Open by appointment only.

Washington College, Chestertown, MD. This small liberal arts college was founded in 1782 in "honorable and perpetual memory of His Excellency General Washington." The college dominates the town with its pretty campus.

Wildfowl Trust of North America (410-827-6694), Wetlands Center, 600 Discovery La., Grasonville, MD.

Lodging

Academy Bed and Breakfast (410-758-2791), 100 Academy La., Centreville, MD 21617. 2 rooms, moderate rates.

Foxley Manor Motel (410-778-3200), 609 Washington Ave., Chestertown, MD 21620.

Hill's Inn (410-778-1926), 114 Washington Ave., Chestertown, MD 21617. Near the college.

Imperial Hotel and Restaurant (410-778-5000), 208 High St., Chestertown, MD 21617. 13 rooms, private baths, expensive.

The White Swan Tavern (410-778-2300), 231 High St., Chestertown, MD 21620. 6 rooms, private baths, moderate rates.

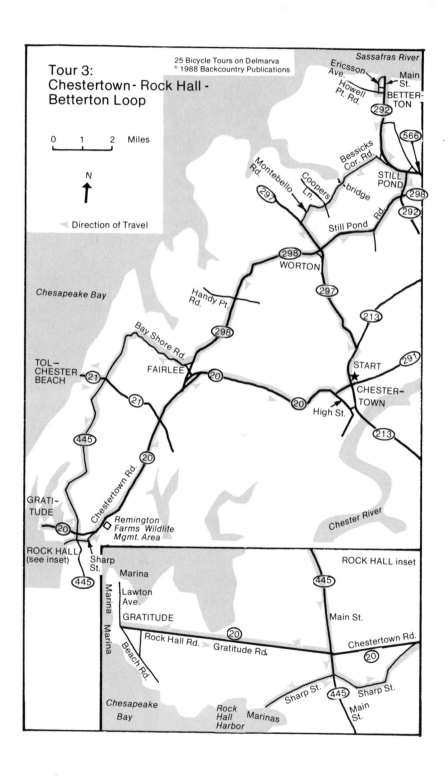

Tour 3:
Chestertown - Rock Hall -
Betterton Loop

25 Bicycle Tours on Delmarva
© 1988 Backcountry Publications

0   1   2   Miles

N

◁ Direction of Travel

Sassafras River

Ericsson Ave.
Howell Pt. Rd.
Main St.
BETTER-TON
292
566

Bessicks Cor. Rd.
STILL POND
298
292

Montebello Rd.
Coopers Ln.
-bridge
297
Still Pond Rd.

298
WORTON
297
213
291

Chesapeake Bay

Handy Pt. Rd.
298

Bay Shore Rd.
FAIRLEE
20
START
CHESTER-TOWN

TOL-CHESTER BEACH
21
21
20
High St.
213

445

20
Chestertown Rd.

GRATI-TUDE
20
Remington Farms Wildlife Mgmt. Area

Chester River

ROCK HALL (see inset)
445
Sharp St.

ROCK HALL inset

Marina
Lawton Ave.
GRATITUDE
Marina
Marina
Beach Rd.
Rock Hall Rd.
Gratitude Rd.
20

445
Main St.
Chestertown Rd.
20

Sharp St.
445
Sharp St.
Main St.

Chesapeake Bay
Rock Hall Harbor
Marinas

3

Chestertown–Rock Hall–Betterton Loop

Distance: *56 miles*
Terrain: *Gently rolling to hilly*
Location: *Kent County, Maryland*
Special features: *Betterton, Rock Hall, views of Chesapeake Bay*

On this tour you are never far from the Chesapeake Bay. Now and then through the trees and across pastures you will have a glimpse of this great body of water. You will travel through some of the prettiest parts of Kent County, Maryland, which contains numerous well-manicured estates and dairy farms. The countryside has a quiet charm reminiscent of England, and I have always been enchanted by its beauty. (I have cycled this loop in both the foulest and the best weather and have come away from the tour convinced that this is one of the best bicycle loops on the Eastern Shore.)

Once the rush-to-work traffic to Chestertown ends around 9 AM, the country roads of this part of Kent County are largely deserted. The one exception is MD 20 (the Rock Hall–Chestertown Road), which has a fair amount of afternoon traffic when seafood trucks from Rock Hall rush the day's catch of crabs, oysters, fish, and clams to urban markets.

The ride starts in Chestertown at the intersection of MD 291 and MD 213 and takes you to Betterton via MD 297, MD 298, and MD 292. From Betterton you will travel on isolated back roads south to Rock Hall and from there on MD 20 north to Chestertown.

Directions for the Ride

0.0   Start at the intersection of MD 291 and MD 213 (Buzz's Restaurant and Foxley Manor Motel). You may leave your car parked in the restaurant's large lot. Proceed north on MD 213.

1.2 Turn left on MD 297 for Betterton.

3.7 Enter Worton, a small Kent village with a well-kept regional park.

4.8 Turn right on MD 298 (Still Pond Road). You'll find Kent County High School at this intersection.

6.7 Stop briefly to examine Friendship, a Chesapeake country manor house built in 1782. Continue through the hamlet of Lynch.

8.5 Bear to the left and continue on MD 292 to Still Pond.

9.1 Still Pond.

This is a charming Kent County village with a country store. Many of the Victorian houses have been restored, and the town has much to delight the eye. For centuries, local inhabitants believed that Still Pond (now a filled-in marsh) was haunted by the ghosts of Native Americans. The name "Still Pond" derives from nearby Still Pond Creek, which was called Steele Pone Creek on August Hermann's famous Maryland map of 1673.

9.4 At the junction of MD 292 and MD 566 turn left and proceed north on MD 292.

12.1 Enter Betterton.

The deteriorated highway that was the bane of cyclists has recently been resurfaced.

13.1 Betterton Beach.

In its heyday, before the opening of the Chesapeake Bay Bridge in 1952, Betterton was a well-known Chesapeake Bay family resort that attracted thousands of day-tripping excursionists. Chesapeake steamboats and ferries would leave Light Street in Baltimore at 8:30 in the morning, deposit their passengers at Betterton, and return to the city in the evening. Today this small Edwardian town is a retreat for those who wish to savor bay breezes at one of the local boardinghouses and swim and fish in the Chesapeake. The beach and park facilities are well maintained. Walk out on the long jetty and you'll have a nice view of the bay and the bluffs of

Betterton. Looking bayward, the large mouth of the Sassafras River is on your right. Plan time for a swim or a picnic on the shady lawns of the park.

As you leave the beach area, take the first right and pedal up Ericsson Avenue, which loops around Betterton. Gear down; this steep hill will test your strength!

13.7 *At the end of Ericsson Avenue turn left on Howell Point Road. This will take you back to MD 292.*

13.9 *At the stop sign on Howell Point Road turn right on MD 292 south.*

16.1 *At the fork of MD 292 turn right on Bessicks Corner Road. Caution: Bessicks Corner Road is not well marked, so take care not to miss it.*

17.7 *Turn left at the stop sign and continue on Bessicks Corner Road. Stop at Still Pond Creek Bridge.*

A Colonial mansion in Chestertown, Maryland (*photo by Orlando V. Wootten*)

The creek will be on your right. This is one of the most impressive tidewater creeks on the Eastern Shore. If you did not know that it was an outlet to Chesapeake Bay, you would call it a large lake.

18.8 *At the intersection of Bessicks Corner Road and Coopers Lane, Bessicks Corner Road takes two name changes—Still Pond Road and Montebello Road.*

20.0 *At the end of Montebello Road turn left on MD 297.*

21.2 *Turn right on MD 298.*

25.0 *At the intersection of Handy Point Road and MD 298 there is a general store, a good place to stop and rest before continuing south to Rock Hall.*

28.0 *Fairlee. Continue through this village and turn right on Bay Shore Road. This route will swing you close to the Chesapeake Bay.*

32.2 *At the intersection of MD 445 and MD 21, turn right and continue on MD 21 to Tolchester.*

Little remains of the once proud resort of Tolchester Beach. Before World War II, however, Tolchester was a premier Chesapeake resort. Owned by the Tolchester Steamship Line, the resort had two hotels, roller coasters, dancing pavilions, and a small lake for boaters. Despite the fenced-in look of the place, you are allowed to walk on the beach and swim.

34.2 *Return back on MD 21 to the junction of MD 21 and MD 445 south. Turn right on MD 445 south.*

39.7 *Enter Rock Hall.*

This town, which proclaims to visitors that "nice people live here," is the seafood capital of Kent County. The town's maritime economy provides employment to a small army of seafood dealers, fishermen, oystermen, crabbers, and restaurant and boatyard workers. Named originally "Rock Haul" for the large numbers of rock fish taken here, the town was also an important terminus on the Annapolis to Philadelphia land-and-water route. Lieutenant Colonel Tench Tilghman passed through Rock Hall in 1781 as he was taking the news of General Cornwallis's surrender at Yorktown, Virginia, to the Continental Congress in Philadelphia. During the

Revolutionary period, Rock Hall was famous for its steamed crabs served at local inns, and Thomas Jefferson and James Madison feasted on them during passages through the area. Today, local restaurants continue this tradition.

40.3 *At the intersection of MD 445 and MD 20, turn right on MD 20 (Rock Hall Road). Notice the large wooden statue of a Chesapeake waterman at the intersection. Continue on MD 20 to the waterfront hamlet of Gratitude. On your right you will pass a small church called the Church Mouse.*

41.9 *This is a port of entry for Chesapeake yachts and pleasure boats. Spend time exploring the marinas. Return on MD 20 to Rock Hall.*

43.5 *Turn right on MD 445; then at the intersection of MD 445 and Sharp Street, turn right on Sharp.*

This street will take you to the marinas of the local bay watermen. Stand on the docks and watch the crabbers and clammers unload their catches and joke with one another. If you can, plan to have the daily special of fried softshelled or steamed hardshelled crabs at the Watermen's Crab House.

44.5 *Proceed back up Sharp Street to MD 445. Turn left on MD 445 and then quickly turn right on MD 20 (Chestertown Road).*

47.0 *Remington Farms Wildlife Management Area.*

In 1957 the Remington Arms Corporation took possession of this game preserve, which was formerly owned by Glenn L. Martin, the aircraft millionaire. The preserve has demonstration programs for raising field crops that provide food and cover for geese and ducks. It is open to the public.

56.0 *Enter Chestertown on MD 20. MD 20 leads right to Chestertown's famous High Street. Follow High Street to the old Customs House and the wharf of the Chester River and the end of a pleasant loop. To return to your car, proceed up High Street and turn right on MD 291, which will take you to the intersection of MD 291 and MD 213 where you began your journey.*

Bicycle Repair Services

Bikework (410-778-6940), 208 Cross St., Chestertown, MD.

Attractions

Durding's Store, 5742 Main St., Rock Hall, MD. An old-fashioned drug-store with an authentic soda fountain. Open daily till 5 PM.

Rock Hall Museum (410-778-1399), South Main Street Municipal Building, Rock Hall, MD. Native American artifacts, nautical relics.

St. Paul's Episcopal Church, 7579 Sandy Bottom Rd., Rock Hall, MD. The oldest continuously used Episcopal church in Maryland. There's a restored 1766 vestry house.

Lodging

Bay Breeze Inn (410-639-2061), 5758 Main St., Rock Hall, MD 21661. 5 rooms, private baths.

Brampton Bed and Breakfast (410-778-1860), 2527 Chestertown Rd. (MD 20), Chestertown, MD 21620. 6 rooms, private baths. Located on a beautiful 35-acre tract with a pond.

Courtyard Inn (410-778-2755), MD 213, South Chestertown, MD 21620. 26 rooms, private baths. Restaurant.

Hill's Inn (410-778-1926), 114 Washington Ave., Chestertown, MD 21620.

The Inn at Mitchell House (410-778-6500), 8796 Maryland Pkwy., Tolchester, MD 21620. 5 rooms, private baths.

Lantern Inn (410-348-5809), 115 Ericsson Ave., Betterton, MD 21610. 13 rooms, private baths.

Mariner's Motel (410-639-2291 or 1-800-787-2291), 5681 Hawthorne Ave., Rock Hall, MD 21661. 12 rooms, private baths.

4

Chestertown, Maryland–New Castle, Delaware

Distance: 52 miles one way
Terrain: Gently rolling with occasional hills
Location: Kent and Cecil Counties, Maryland; New Castle County, Delaware
Special features: Kitty Knight House, Sassafras River, Bohemia River, Chesapeake City, New Castle

From Chestertown northward the countryside becomes more rolling and the landscape is dotted with numerous dairy farms. Names on country byways like Clabber Road and Creamery Lane attest to the importance of the dairy industry in Kent County.

Heading north on MD 213, this ride will take you through the Sassafras River country. Named for the tree with its famous medicinal bark, the Sassafras is considered by many to be one of the most beautiful rivers on the Delmarva Peninsula. Unlike the marshy tidal rivers of the southern Eastern Shore, the Sassafras is high banked and well defined. Atop gentle slopes that lead to the water's edge, you can spy some of the proudest old estates and plantations in Maryland. Captain John Smith sailed up the Sassafras in 1607 and named it Tockwogh after the Algonquian-family tribe that lived here.

During the War of 1812, the Sassafras was an important artery of the grain trade for the American forces. On May 5, 1813, British Admiral George Cockburn sailed up the Sassafras in the HMS *Marlborough* with a flotilla of small boats and 150 marines and burned the twin villages of Georgetown and Fredericktown.

Continuing northward into Cecil County, you will ride across land that once was part of the 25,000-acre Bohemia Manor of August Her-

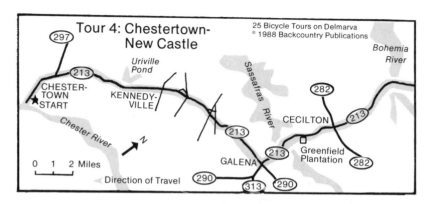

mann, the famous 17th-century map maker. After crossing the Bohemia River, you will soon arrive in Chesapeake City. A delightful village on the Chesapeake and Delaware Canal, Chesapeake City was a thriving canal port in the 19th and early 20th centuries. Nearby is the popular Chesapeake and Delaware Canal Museum.

Crossing the peninsula in a northeasterly direction, you arrive at the final destination of this tour, New Castle, Delaware. This tastefully preserved colonial center is reminiscent of Williamsburg, Virginia, and was the first capital of Delaware. For two centuries New Castle played an important role in the economy of the Delaware River area.

Directions for the Ride

0.0 *Depart Chestertown at the Foxley Manor Hotel (where you can leave your car if you are not having someone drive it to pick you up in New Castle) on Washington Avenue and proceed due north on MD 213.*

5.0 *Uriville Pond is on the left.*

This is one of the many ponds and lakes created in the region by the New Deal WPA in the 1930s.

7.8 *Kennedyville is an important dairy center in Kent County and home of a small but thriving Amish community.*

10.5 *Historical marker and birthplace of General John Cadwalader.*

Cadwalader was a close friend of General George Washington and

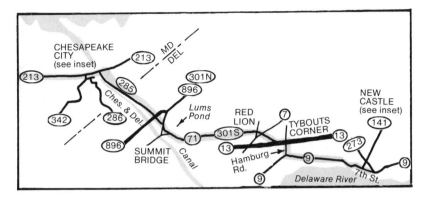

a Revolutionary War patriot. When he learned of the Conway Cabal to depose Washington as commander in chief, Cadwalader challenged General Thomas Conway to a duel and wounded him in the mouth. Cadwalader subsequently boasted, "I have stopped that damned rascal's lying tongue at any rate."

15.3 Galena.

During the American Revolution, Galena was an important way station on the land and water route from Philadelphia to Annapolis. George Washington stopped here on his way to and from the first Continental Congress in 1774.

At Galena you will come to the junction of MD 213, MD 290, and MD 313. As you approach the traffic light at the intersection, Billy's Restaurant will be on your right. Turn left at the intersection and continue on MD 213.

17.0 Kitty Knight House.

Now a famous inn on a bluff overlooking the Sassafras River, the Kitty Knight House is named for an intrepid woman who stood up to Admiral Cockburn's invading forces in May 1813. According to local history, Kitty Knight extinguished fires in two houses with her broom as fast as the British soldiers lit them until a sympathetic officer ordered that these two houses be spared. The rear deck and patio of this inn afford a spectacular view of the Sassafras River.

18.0 Sassafras River Bridge. *Plan to gear your bike down while crossing the bridge, as you will have to climb a steep hill.*

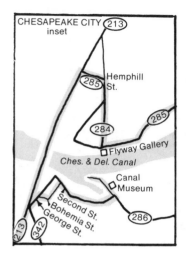

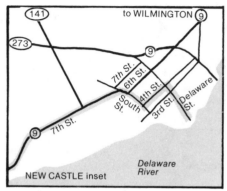

20.0 Grenfield Plantation.

This estate was patented by John and Mary Ward in 1674. The Georgian mansion that dominates the landscape was built in the 1740s and is a good example of the kind of Chesapeake manor house that existed in the region before the American Revolution.

20.2 Cecilton is a small crossroads hamlet and convenient resting point.

Like all the places bearing the name of Cecil in this region, the hamlet of Cecilton was named for Cecilius Calvert, the second Lord Baltimore.

21.8 The Anchorage, on your left.

This estate belonged to the famous Lusby family of 18th-century Maryland and was the home of Commodore Jacob Jones and his wife, Ruth Lusby. Jones commanded the United States naval sloop *Wasp* and was a hero of the War of 1812. The mansion is a fine example of Chesapeake country "telescope" architecture.

24.5 Bohemia River.

This river is named for the home province of August Hermann, a native of Prague, who settled in Maryland in the 17th century. In the 1680s August Hermann was awarded 25,000 acres of land in payment for surveying the province of Maryland. The survey project took nearly 10 years, and the August Hermann map enabled the Lords Baltimore to defend their proprietorship in court against the encroachments of Pennsylvania and Virginia.

30.0 *Chesapeake City. Turn right on MD 286 to South Chesapeake City.*

30.4 *Enter Chesapeake City on George Street and turn right on Bohemia Street. Straight ahead lies the Chesapeake and Delaware Canal. At the intersection of Bohemia and Second Streets, turn right onto Second Street to proceed to the canal museum.*

31.6 *Chesapeake and Delaware Canal Museum.*

The road loops around salt marsh and offers a good view of the canal, Chesapeake City, and the canal bridge. As early as 1661 August Hermann had dreamed of a canal that would connect Chesapeake Bay with the Delaware River, but it was not until 1764 that surveying began. The digging of the canal commenced in 1804, and the canal was formally opened for business in 1829. As the Chesapeake Bay was 7 feet higher than the Delaware River, the canal was built with several locks. The old steam engine and waterwheel that pumped water into the first lock are on display in the canal museum. The canal was purchased by the federal government in 1919 and enlarged. Today the Chesapeake and Delaware Canal offers a route that saves Baltimore-bound vessels on the Delaware from the long 400-mile trip down the Atlantic coast and up the Chesapeake.

32.7 *Bridge over the Chesapeake and Delaware Canal.*

Traffic is heavy on this narrow bridge, so walk your bike across the high mile-long span on the right-hand sidewalk. For those who are not squeamish, the view of the canal and surrounding area is excellent.

33.8 *At the end of the bridge turn right on MD 285 (Hemphill Street), which will take you into North Chesapeake City.*

34.2 *Turn right on MD 284.*

34.4 *Turn left at the T-intersection and stop sign onto MD 285. You will be facing the Flyway Gallery. Continue on MD 285, which*

The author in Chesapeake City, Maryland

parallels the Chesapeake and Delaware Canal.

38.9 *A half mile after you ride across the Summit Bridge overpass turn right on DE 71. This road is an isolated stretch of highway and is not well marked.*

39.6 *Lums Pond State Park camping area.*

At this point you will have crossed into Delaware; Lums Pond is the state's largest lake. It was built by the state as a water source for the Chesapeake and Delaware Canal lock pumps.

After Lums Pond State Park, DE 71 becomes US 301 South.

45.0 *Hamlet of Red Lion and junction of DE 7 and US 301 South. Continue north on US 301 South.*

46.0 *Junction of US 301S and US 13 at Tybouts Corner. Turn left on US 13 North. US 13 is a busy four-lane highway, so proceed with caution on the shoulder for 0.5 mile.*

46.7 *Turn right at the stoplight intersection of US 13 and Hamburg Road. Jack's Buffet Restaurant and a gas station will be on your right. Turn right on Hamburg Road and proceed to DE 9.*

52.2 *Turn left on DE 9. Then continue straight into New Castle on Seventh Street. At the intersection of Seventh and South Streets, turn right on South Street. Turn left on Fourth Street, which leads directly to Delaware Street and the heart of historic New Castle.*

52.6 *New Castle historic area.*

New Castle, first named Fort Casimir, was founded in 1651 by the Dutch under Peter Stuyvesant. Its location at a bend in the Delaware gave New Castle command of the river traffic. The flags of Sweden, the Netherlands, and Great Britain have flown at the Old Court House near the square. New Castle is also the site where William Penn landed in October 1682 to accept the New World grant of Pennsylvania from the Duke of York. While many of the old Georgian mansions are in private ownership, several buildings, including the Old Court House and Amstel House, are open to the public.

Bike down Delaware Street to the Battery along the Delaware River. After this long day's ride, you might prefer to take a leisurely walk through this enchanting town.

Note: New Castle is also a convenient departure point for those who wish to continue into Wilmington and northward into the Brandywine Valley.

A Note for the Return Ride

This tour complements Tour 5, and ambitious cyclists may wish to push on to Lewes, Delaware. If New Castle is the end of your journey, plan to be met by a car or van. For informa-

tion about bus service for you and your bike to other destinations, call Greyhound Bus Lines, 1-800-528-0447.

Bicycle Repair Services

The Bike Barn (302-328-8975), 500 School La., New Castle, DE.

Attractions

Amstel House Museum (302-322-2794). Built in 1730 and located at Fourth and Delaware Streets in New Castle, the museum displays colonial arts and handicrafts. Open Tuesday through Saturday 11–4.

The Old Court House (302-571-3059). New Castle was Delaware's capital for many years. The 1732 courthouse is now a museum featuring several portraits of signers of the Declaration of Independence. Open Tuesday through Saturday 10–4:30, Sunday 1–4:30.

The town of New Castle, Delaware, hosts an annual Day in Old New Castle on the third Saturday of May. Twenty private houses and some lovely old gardens are opened to the public at this time.

Lodging

The Anchorage B&B (410-275-1972), PO Box 575, Cecilton, MD 21913. 5 rooms, private baths.

The Blue Max Inn (410-885-2781), 300 S. Bohemia Ave., Chesapeake City, MD 21915. 7 rooms, private baths.

Bohemia House (410-885-3024), 1236 Town Point Rd., Chesapeake City, MD 21915. 9 rooms, private baths.

Chesapeake City B&B (410-885-2200), 208 Bank St., Chesapeake City, MD 21915. 5 rooms, private baths.

David Finney Inn (302-322-6367), 216 Delaware St., New Castle, DE 19720.

Granvier-Black House B&B (302-328-1339), 17 The Strand, New Castle, DE 19720. 5 rooms, private baths.

Inn at the Canal (410-885-5995), 104 Bohemia Ave., Chesapeake City, MD 21915. 6 rooms, private baths.

William Penn Guest House (302-328-7736), 206 Delaware St., New Castle, DE 19720.

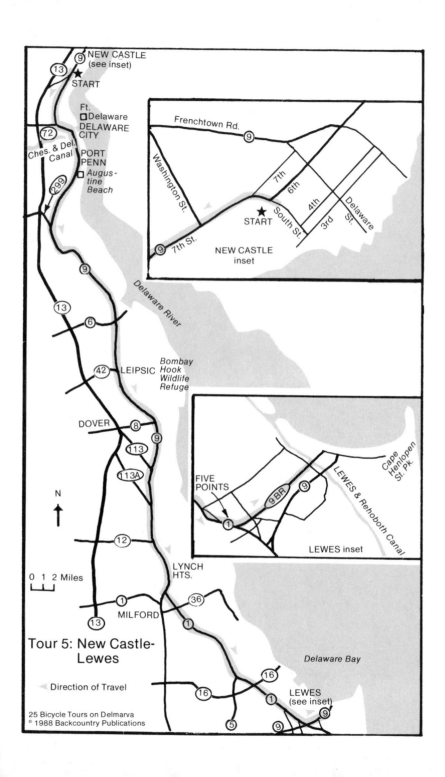

NEW CASTLE
(see inset)

START

Ft.
Delaware
DELAWARE
CITY

PORT
PENN
Augus-
tine
Beach

Ches. & Del. Canal

Frenchtown Rd.

Washington St.

7th
6th
4th
3rd

Delaware St.

START
South St.

7th St.

NEW CASTLE
inset

Delaware River

Bombay
Hook
Wildlife
Refuge

LEIPSIC

DOVER

FIVE
POINTS

9 BR

LEWES & Rehoboth Canal

Cape
Henlopen
St. Pk.

LEWES inset

N

0 1 2 Miles

LYNCH
HTS.

MILFORD

Tour 5: New Castle-
Lewes

Direction of Travel

Delaware Bay

LEWES
(see inset)

25 Bicycle Tours on Delmarva
© 1988 Backcountry Publications

5

New Castle–Lewes

Distance: *89 miles one way*
Terrain: *Gently rolling to flat*
Location: *New Castle, Kent, and Sussex Counties, Delaware*
Special features: *Delaware City, Port Penn, Augustine Beach, Dover Air Force Base, Lewes*

You will find some of the best and worst cycling in southern Delaware on this trip. DE 9 winds lazily south through the marshes of the Delaware River, and the nature preserves at Augustine Fish and Wildlife Area and the Bombay Hook Nature Preserve guarantee that this route will continue to be one of the loveliest on the Delmarva Peninsula. You can stop and swim at Augustine Beach or watch birds or the numerous muskrats at work. In late May and early June the marshes are a festival of color, with dozens of species of wildflowers in bloom. For the most part, you will be at peace with yourself on this trip as DE 9 has little traffic, especially during the week. The only unwelcome specter on your horizon will be the Salem nuclear power facility across the Delaware River in New Jersey. Its ominous presence contrasts starkly with the beauty of DE 9.

Continuing south, you will enter Delaware City, an old canal port with a restored inn and a battery park overlooking the Delaware River. Once you pass the village of Leipsic (pronounced "lipsick" by locals), you will be in the more trafficked area of Dover. You won't have to look for Dover Air Force Base; it will be all around you. Planes will be constantly flying overhead as the base is the home of the Military Airlift Command, the main troop and transport terminal for the United States armed forces in Europe. South of Dover the trip becomes boring, and the principal objective is to get to Lewes as quickly as possible. US 113 and DE

1 are four-lane highways that offer a minimally decent shoulder for cyclists. In the summer this will be the hot part of your trip, so stop often to rest and take fluids.

One final note: Despite the signs that say "Visit Historic Milford," the town should be avoided. The traffic patterns are confusing, the roads are poor, and the town is nondescript. Your time is much better spent on the beach at Lewes or Cape Henlopen.

Directions for the Ride

0.0 *From South Street in New Castle turn left onto DE 9 South. Leaving New Castle, the highway has two lanes and heavy traffic in the morning. Use caution.*

6.3 *On your right you will pass the Occidental Chemical Corporation.*

Hold your nose and think of the great ride that awaits you.

7.7 *At the junction of DE 72, motorists turn right to get out to US 13 and you will have DE 9 South all to yourself.*

9.7 *Enter Delaware City. Turn left on Clinton Street and head directly for Battery Park.*

10.4 *Battery Park and Olde Canal Inn.*

In the 19th century, Delaware was the prosperous eastern terminus of the Chesapeake and Delaware Canal and was also the home port of the Delaware fishing fleet. Delaware City reflected a boomtown spirit characteristic of many ports in the Chesapeake Bay region at that time.

By 1917 the town's fate had been sealed by the decision of the United States Army Corps of Engineers to construct a new outlet to the canal several miles south of Delaware City that would allow for passage of larger ships. The town's canal economy went into decline and Delaware City became a seedy backwater village. Today, however, it has become popular with tourists. The town is undergoing modest gentrification, and the restored Battery Park offers a splendid view of the Delaware River. Many people picnic here and spend hours watching the oceangoing vessels heading for Wilmington and Philadelphia.

Lewes, Delaware (*photo by Orlando V. Wootten*)

Historically, Delaware City's principal claim to fame has rested on its having been the site of a Civil War fortress and prison camp. Fort Delaware was located on Pea Patch Island in the shipping channel of the Delaware River. Thirty-two-pound seacoast artillery cannons protected the river from marauding Confederate vessels, and the massive stone structure of the fortress is now a museum. Confederate prisoners were housed there during the war.

From the wharf on the old canal near the Battery, you can take a boat out to the fort at 11 AM on the weekend from late April through September.

You can leave Delaware City either by retracing your route out Clinton Street or by following the road along the old canal (now a favorite mooring site for pleasure boats). Either way, it is 1 mile back to DE 9, where you will turn left. Just outside Delaware City you cross a bridge over the Chesapeake and Delaware Canal.

On a clear day the view of the canal, the Delaware Bay, and the surrounding countryside is spectacular. On your left from the bridge you will see the current base of the Army Corps of Engineers, which is responsible for maintaining the canal and the ship channels of the Delaware River.

15.1 ***Port Penn on the Delaware River lies at the head of Delaware Bay.***

Tradition has it that William Penn, the founder of Pennsylvania, once landed there for fresh water. Earlier in this century Port Penn was the home port of an extensive shad and sturgeon fishing fleet. Today it is a charming country village. Stop for hot dogs and coffee at the village market. Also, if time permits, visit Port Penn Museum.

Continue south on DE 9.

16.0 ***Augustine Beach.***

Today little remains of Augustine Beach, once a popular resort with bars, a dance hall, and a hotel. The beach offers good vistas of the Delaware River, however, and is still popular with local fishermen. The beach was named for August Hermann, the famous surveyor of Maryland and Delaware, who made a map for Cecilius Calvert, the second Lord Baltimore, in 1662. In the fall, the wildlife preserve here is filled with thousands of Canada geese.

18.3 ***Augustine Fish and Wildlife Area.***

19.0 ***Plank bridge across a marsh creek. The bridge is old and the nail studs are sticking up. To avoid a flat, dismount and walk your bike across the bridge.***

20.9 ***The Colonial mansion Knowlbush Haven, circa 1780.***

This is one of a few plantations built close to the marsh. Now salt marshes and tidal ponds begin to give way to honeysuckle and corn that sprouts 8 feet into the air.

22.7 ***At the intersection of DE 299 and DE 9, the road forms a T. Go left on DE 9.***

32.0 ***Fleming's Landing Bridge.***

This bridge in the past has been closed to traffic because of its deplorable condition. It has been repaired recently, however, and it is a pleasure to cross it.

41.0 ***Leipsic. Cycle through the village, which is worth a quick visit.***

This old fishing and oystering town sits at the edge of the largest tidal marsh area in Delaware.

52.4 *At the outskirts of Dover Air Force Base, DE 9 ends. Head south on US 113.*

64.4 *Village of Lynch Heights.*

If you do not wish to push on to Lewes, there is a Colony Inn and Restaurant here where you can spend the night.

65.4 *Turn left on DE 1 to Lewes. Unfortunately, this four-lane ocean highway is the only route you can take. It is a busy road in the summer, but there is a wide shoulder to cycle on. Use caution.*

89.0 *Lewes, Delaware. You will enter Lewes at the busy intersection known as Five Points. Turn left on US 9BR and proceed into Lewes. Be careful, as there is a lot of traffic in the summer, and vacationers, especially those pulling boats and trailers, seem to be blind when it comes to cyclists.*

A Note for the Return Ride

For the return trip to New Castle you can either retrace your route by bike or arrange to be met by car or van in Lewes. Considering the distance involved, I strongly suggest the latter alternative.

Bicycle Repair Services

Bike Etc. (302-422-8030), 3 N. Walnut St., Milford, DE.

Campers Corner/Bike Barn (302-328-8975), 500 School La., New Castle, DE.

Attractions

Old Colonial Lewes, Delaware. Cycle past Colonial homes on Third and Ship Carpenter Streets. The Lewes Historical Society Museum (302-645-8988) is located here as well; open Memorial Day through Labor Day,

An inland waterway in Lewes, Deleware (*photo by Orlando V. Wootten*)

Tuesday through Saturday 10–4. The museum hosts a crafts fair in mid-July.

Lodging

Cape Henlopen Motel (302-645-2828), Savannah and Anglers Rds., Lewes, DE 19958.

Colony Inn at Lynch Heights (302-422-2777), US 113 and DE 1, Milford, DE 19963.

New Devon Inn (302-322-6367), Second and Market Sts., Lewes, DE 19958. 17 rooms, private baths.

6
Lewes, Delaware–Fenwick Island

Distance: *28.5 miles one way*
Terrain: *Beach dunes and flat highway*
Location: *Sussex County, Delaware*
Special features: *Lewes, Rehoboth Beach, Delaware state beaches, Fenwick Island Light House*

For the beach lover, this is the ultimate bicycle excursion. The tour takes you through the lovely seaside towns of Lewes, Rehoboth Beach, and Bethany Beach. These towns are known as the quiet resorts of Delmarva, and you will find little of the tourist pollution, neon, and tinsel characteristic of the Ocean City mega-resort to the south. In fact, this trip is designed to end on Fenwick Island at the northern boundary of Ocean City. From there, if you like, proceed south into the traffic-bound expanse of condominiums. My advice is to stay north in Delaware and enjoy the quiet resorts and the still-unspoiled state beaches of Delaware. Admittedly, there has been some development, especially at Dewey Beach and Bethany Beach, but it has not become grotesque yet.

Lewes, Delaware, has been an interesting coastal spot since Henry Hudson first sailed into the Delaware Bay in 1609. In the 17th century, the Dutch planted a whaling colony on Lewes Creek, but the settlers were massacred by Native Americans. The Dutch resettled the Lewes area until 1664, when the English gained control of the Delaware colony.

In the past, Lewes was of strategic military importance because it stood at the Delaware Bay gateway. Since the colonial period, it has been the home of the highly skilled Delaware Bay ship pilots, who help vessels navigate up the Delaware Bay and the Delaware River to Philadelphia.

Lewes found itself in the center of conflict during the War of 1812,

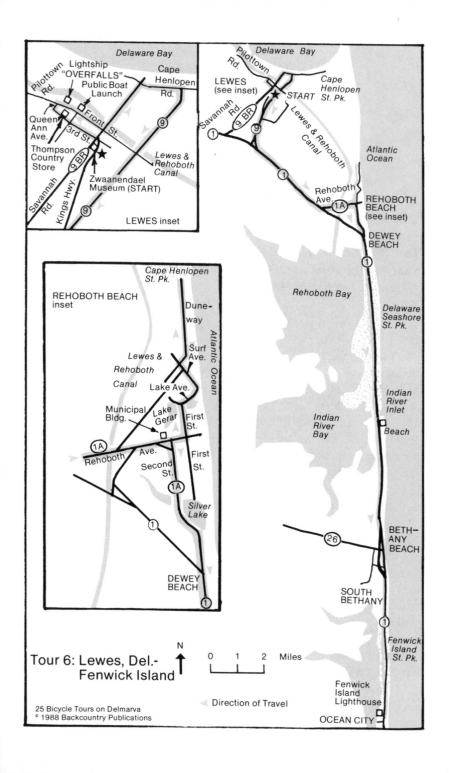

Delaware Bay

Lightship
"OVERFALLS"
Public Boat
Launch

Pilottown Rd.

Cape
Henlopen
Rd.

Front St.

Queen
Ann
Ave.

3rd St.

9 BR

Thompson
Country
Store

Savannah Rd.

Kings Hwy.

9

Zwaanendael
Museum (START)

Lewes &
Rehoboth
Canal

9

LEWES inset

Delaware Bay

Pilottown Rd.

LEWES
(see inset)

START

Cape
Henlopen
St. Pk.

Savannah Rd.

9 BR

9

Lewes & Rehoboth Canal

Atlantic
Ocean

1

1

Rehoboth
Ave.

1A

REHOBOTH
BEACH
(see inset)

DEWEY
BEACH

1

Rehoboth Bay

Delaware
Seashore
St. Pk.

REHOBOTH BEACH
inset

Cape Henlopen
St. Pk.

Dune-
way

Lewes &
Rehoboth
Canal

Surf
Ave.

Lake Ave.

Atlantic
Ocean

Municipal
Bldg.

Lake
Gerar

First
St.

1A

Rehoboth

Ave.

First
St.

Second
St.

1A

Silver
Lake

1

DEWEY
BEACH

1

Indian
River
Bay

Indian
River
Inlet

Beach

BETH-
ANY
BEACH

26

SOUTH
BETHANY

1

Fenwick
Island
St. Pk.

Tour 6: Lewes, Del.-
Fenwick Island

N

0   1   2   Miles

◄ Direction of Travel

Fenwick
Island
Lighthouse

OCEAN CITY

25 Bicycle Tours on Delmarva
© 1988 Backcountry Publications

and British naval vessels bombarded the town in April 1813. Throughout the 19th century, Lewes was a favorite port for Atlantic coasting schooners. When the railroad came to town in 1869, Lewes became a major fish-processing center. Since the 1890s, Lewes has been a small but popular resort. The town is dotted with saltbox Colonial houses and has a large community of affluent retired citizens. Given the moderate climate, the Colonial charm of the town, and access to the beaches of Delaware, property values have skyrocketed.

A short distance from Lewes is Cape Henlopen State Park, a 2500-acre reserve of surf and sand, seabirds, unusual flora, and winding nature trails. Many cyclists camp at the state campground here, a favorite launching point to catch the nearby Lewes Ferry for Cape May, New Jersey. Throughout the park and along the Delaware coast, you will see huge pipelike towers above the sand dunes. These are remains of World War II bunkers, gun placements, and observation towers. During the war, German submarines were often sighted off the Delaware coast. Today the state has refurbished one of the observation towers in the park, and you can climb the 115 stairs to the top for a grand view of Cape Henlopen State Park and the surrounding beaches.

Directions for the Ride

0.0 *Given the Dutch history of Lewes, our trip begins appropriately at the Zwaanendael Museum at the intersection of King's Highway and Savannah Road. You can park your car here.*

A replica of the Town Hall in Hoorn, Holland, the Zwaanendael Museum was erected by the state of Delaware in 1931 to commemorate the 300th anniversary of the founding of the Dutch settlement here. The name "Zwaanendael" means "valley of the swans," and the leader of the Dutch, David Pieterson de Vries, was born in Hoorn. The museum contains many interesting artifacts that reflect on Lewes's early history.

0.3 *Lewes Historic Complex. From the front of the museum, go left on Third Street.*

You are cycling past a popular historic complex of Colonial homes and shops that have been carefully restored. While many of these structures are private residences, some are open to the public. The

The Zwaanendael Museum in Lewes, Delaware

Thompson Country Store (built in 1800) is open daily and has a small handicraft and gift shop.

Continue on Third Street to Queen Anne Avenue.

0.5 **At the stop sign and intersection of Queen Avenue and Third Street, turn right onto Pilottown Road.**

In the 19th century this area of Lewes was the neighborhood of the Delaware Bay pilots. Today many pilots continue to live in these well-kept Victorian residences.

0.7 **Lewes public boat landing area is on your left, and there is a good view of the town marina and the Lewes-Rehoboth Canal.**

The lightship *Overfalls* is moored nearby. Until the 1950s, this boat anchored over Overfalls Shoals off the coast to warn away commercial ships. The lightship is now a museum located between Queen and Park Avenues on Pilottown Road.

0.9 *Pilottown Road becomes Front Street. Turn left at the traffic light and cross the drawbridge. You will now be on Savannah Road.*

1.4 *Turn right on Cape Henlopen Road and follow the signs to the Cape May–Lewes Ferry and Cape Henlopen State Park.*

It is ironic that although Lewes receives ferryloads of motoring visitors every hour, many if not most of these visitors depart quickly without visiting Lewes or Cape Henlopen. There are plenty of paved roads in Cape Henlopen, and at the entrances to the beach there are bike racks where you can secure your bicycle.

1.8 *Just before entering Cape Henlopen State Park, turn right on US 9. This will take you west out of Lewes so that you can catch the main road to Rehoboth Beach.*

2.4 *Cross the bridge on US 9 over the Lewes-Rehoboth Canal.*

4.9 *At the traffic light and intersection of DE 1 and US 9, turn left on DE 1.*

8.4 *Exit left at the traffic light into Rehoboth Beach. In the summer, the traffic is tricky at these intersections, and the highway shoulder is often a curse more than anything else.*

Delaware roads are poorly maintained! You will know when to turn left to go to Rehoboth when you see the Playland Park and Giant Elephant on your right. So . . . turn left at the elephant! You will be on DE 1A.

9.4 *Rehoboth Beach Municipal Building. DE 1A becomes Rehoboth Avenue. Proceed straight ahead to the beach and boardwalk.*

The town library will be on your right, and it's a nice place to stop and rest or browse through a magazine. Directly across the street, the Municipal Building offers tourist information.

Compared to the sprawl and noise of other Atlantic resorts, Rehoboth is civilized—very civilized. But there is evidence of its popularity with nearby metropolitan residents: The beaches may look like volleyball courts, and property values have gone out of sight. The town, however, is true to its strict Methodist heritage. Families and children dominate the boardwalk, and the concession stands are fewer in number and less garish than at other resorts. You can bike on the boardwalk in the morning before 10 AM.

Rehoboth Beach is a year-round community that rests comfortably back from the ocean in stands of loblolly pine. The town's name gives it away, for "Rehoboth," as taken from the book of Genesis in the Bible, means "room enough," and there is certainly room enough for cyclists in this resort. Relax and cycle through quiet neighborhoods. Two blocks away from the boardwalk it is hard to believe that you are at Delaware's major resort.

SIDE TRIP: One of my favorite bicycle jaunts in Rehoboth is to head north on First Street past Lake Gerar, turning right on Lake Avenue. Then turn left on Surf Avenue. Follow this thoroughfare into Duneway and you will find a very pleasant neighborhood that is close by the sea, yet discreetly tucked away in a pine forest. At the end of the road you will be at the southern boundary of Cape Henlopen State Park.

The town of Rehoboth Beach has more than 15 parks and plenty of lakes and ponds. If you tire of the 1.1-mile boardwalk, there will still be plenty to see and do.

If you are a beach purist and hate crowds, then head south out of town for Delaware Seashore State Park, which contains 7 miles of unspoiled beach and facilities for swimming, fishing, camping, and boating. In the off-season you will occasionally see nude bathers here.

9.5 *From Rehoboth Avenue head south on Second Street. Merge into DE 1A.*

10.1 *Silver Lake.*

This is one of Rehoboth's best freshwater ponds. Given the lush greenery, the bird life, the lake, and the sea, Silver Lake Shores is a swanky development.

12.2 *In Dewey Beach, DE 1A and DE 1 merge. After passing through Dewey Beach, home of the summer party and nightclub set, you will come to Delaware Seashore State Park. The beaches are patrolled by lifeguards, and there are showers,* toilets, and ample supplies of fresh drinking water. South of Dewey Beach begins the stretch of DE 1 that will take you cruising for miles along the sand dunes of the Atlantic and the placid waters of Rehoboth Bay.

16.8 *Indian River Inlet. Cross the high bridge over the inlet carefully.*

You'll have a splendid view of the sea and Indian River Bay. Use the sidewalk on Indian River Inlet Bridge; it's safer.

17.6 *Indian River Inlet Beach is on your left.*

Showers and fresh water are available at this guarded beach.

21.6 *Turn left into Bethany Beach off DE 1. The street is unmarked, but turn left at the Delaware National Guard and the Exxon station.*

Bethany Beach is a good place to stop and rest for lunch.

22.1 *At the intersection of Garfield and Pennsylvania Streets turn left to go to the beach or turn right to go back out to DE 1. Turn left (south) on DE 1.*

24.7 *Fenwick Island State Park.*

This is the last state beach before Ocean City, so use it to advantage as you will soon be entering the condominium and private beach belt of north Ocean City.

28.3 *Turn right on 146th Street to the Fenwick Island Light House.*

Surprisingly the lighthouse is located on the bay side of the island.

28.5 Built in 1858 to warn ships away from the Fenwick Shoals, the lighthouse was once the largest building at Fenwick. Now the 89-foot structure is dwarfed by high-rise apartment buildings. Architecturally, Fenwick Island Light House is perhaps one of the best-designed structures of this type in the region. Before switching to kerosene in the 1880s, the light burned whale oil.

A Note for the Return Ride

I suggest retracing your path back to Rehoboth Beach, which is exactly what my son Stewart and I did. It is a direct route

and relatively free of traffic. However, if you wish, you can continue south on DE I to the southern tip of Ocean City and then across Assowoman Bay Bridge on US 50. Right after the bridge you can pick up the route described from Salisbury in Tour 27 and head west.

In summer, no doubt, you'll be swimming in the Atlantic. Take care to shower well, as sand in the critical areas of the body can cause a very uncomfortable ride.

Bicycle Repair Services

Sundancer (410-289-3516), S. Baltimore Ave., Ocean City, MD.

Continental Cycles, Inc. (410-524-1313), 7203 Coastal Hwy., Ocean City, MD.

Attractions

Cape Henlopen State Park (302-645-8983), 42 Cape Henlopen Dr., Lewes, DE 19558. Just outside of Lewes, this park occupies a sandy hook with ocean and bay views on both sides. Camping facilities are available. There is a pier for crabbing and fishing. The park has a nine-hole Frisbee golf course.

Lodging

Corner Cupboard Inn (302-227-8553), 50 Park Ave., Rehoboth Beach, DE 19971. Expensive but breakfast and dinner are included.

Fenwick Inn (1-800-492-1873), 13801 Coastal Hwy., Ocean City, MD 21842. 200 rooms, swimming pool, and hot tub.

Taylor House Bed and Breakfast (410-289-1177), 1001 Baltimore Ave., Ocean City, MD 21812. 4 rooms, shared and private baths. Advertised as serving "one of the best breakfasts of your life!"

Note: If you wish to spend more than 3 days in the area, you may be better off renting a condominium from Rehoboth Resort Realty, 302-227-6116.

7

Lewes, Delaware–Cape May, New Jersey

Distance: *17 nautical miles across Delaware Bay, 20 miles cycling in Cape May*
Terrain: *Flat to rolling countryside*
Location: *Sussex County, Delaware; Cape May County, New Jersey*
Special features: *Lewes–Cape May Ferry, Cape May*
Caution: *Heavy beach traffic in summer*

This tour will take you off the Delmarva Peninsula and out of Chesapeake Bay country, but the ferry ride across Delaware Bay is so glorious and the town of Cape May so intriguing that the trip is well worth it.

In Cape May you will be able to combine a day at the beach with a tour of the bygone Victorian era. The architecture of Cape May makes it one of the loveliest mid-Atlantic ocean resorts. A National Landmark Town since 1976, Cape May has many "gingerbread" Victorian homes, cottages, and guest houses that lend this resort a distinctive charm lacking in more raucous beach towns like Ocean City.

Cape May is located on a peninsula that stretches some 20 miles seaward. It was an early port for whaling ships, an important commercial fishing center, and it has been a popular summer resort since early in the 19th century. The large hotels were the sites of numerous balls for Baltimore debutantes; Wallis Warfield, the future wife of the Duke of Windsor, came out in Cape May.

The Victorian village atmosphere of Cape May also conveys yesteryear's strong sense of family, and Cape May is still very much a family resort. No college high jinks or motorcycle crowds are welcome here! Unlike many resorts, accommodations are reasonably priced. An open-

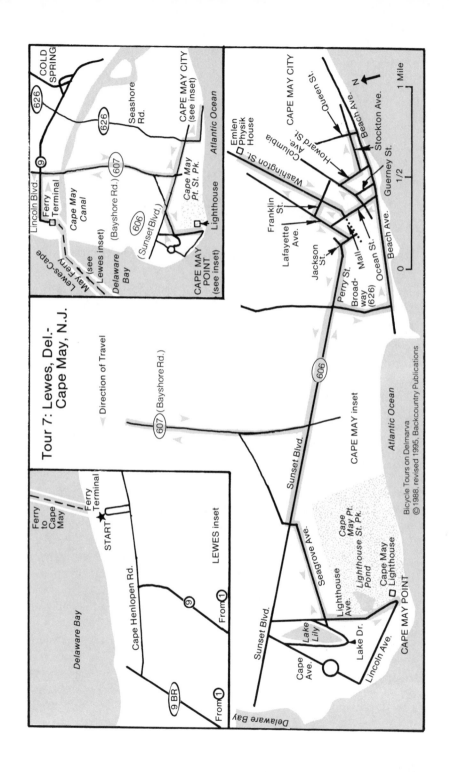

Tour 7: Lewes, Del.-
Cape May, N.J.

Direction of Travel

Bicycle Tours on Delmarva
©1988, revised 1995, Backcountry Publications

air mall in the center of town is lined with shops and sidewalk cafés. On a summer day, my wife and I spent a pleasant 2 hours dining and people-watching on the mall.

During the tourist season (Memorial Day through Labor Day), Cape May is a chore to navigate on a bicycle. After trying to get through the crowds, my wife and I gave up and parked our bikes in one of the many conveniently located steel bike racks. From the mall, it is a 2-block walk to the beach promenade. Also at the mall, the Cape May Historical Society distributes brochures for a historic walking tour of the town. There are more than 600 Victorian houses in Cape May, and as you follow the walking tour, you may find yourself wondering about those 19th-century residents who used the hitching posts and carriage steps and gossiped on the large Victorian porches and verandas.

Directions for the Ride

0.0   *Park your car in the Lewes–Cape May Ferry terminal parking lot at Lewes, Delaware. It is 1 mile east of the town on the way to Cape Henlopen State Park on US 9BR. Do not let the large number of cars in the parking lot in the summer discourage you; there is always room for a cyclist and a bike on board.*

Purchase your tickets at the outside booths, and line up in the special bike lane. You will probably find yourself among a large group, as the ferry is extremely popular with day-tripping bikers. This is an excellent time to talk shop with cyclists about equipment, places to see, campsites, and the joys and problems of the road ahead.

As you board the ferry, you will be directed to park your bike inside the steel bumper lanes. I suggest that you lock your bike to the steel bumper and take your saddlebags with you to the upper decks. This large ferry carries many passengers, and it is better to be safe than sorry. If you are planning to stay only for the day in Cape May, check the ferry schedule. Nothing ruins a relaxing day at the beach like a fast sprint to catch the last ferry back to Lewes.

The Lewes–Cape May Ferry runs 7 days a week, and until September 17 during the tourist season there is a ferry nearly

65

every hour. Check the ferry schedule for details. For further information, call the terminal in Lewes, Delaware, at 302-645-6313.

The trip from the ferry terminal to Cape May is an easy jaunt.

0.0 *Cape May, New Jersey, ferry terminal. From the ferry proceed along US 9 South (Lincoln Boulevard).*

1.0 *Turn right onto Bay Shore Road (NJ 607). Proceed southwest, crossing the Cape May Canal.*

3.5 *Bay Shore Road forks. Follow the left (south) fork to Sunset Boulevard (NJ 606) and make a left.*

4.5 *Turn right onto Broadway (NJ 626) and enter Cape May. Broadway is Cape May's main thoroughfare; it takes you to both the downtown mall area and the beach.*

The easiest way to see Cape May is to follow Broadway to the beach and then turn left on Beach Avenue. After 0.5 mile, turn left on Ocean Street, which will take you into the heart of Cape May's historic district. At 0.3 mile, turn right on Columbia Avenue.

On this delightful, tree-lined avenue are many carefully restored Victorian bed & breakfast inns. At 635 Columbia Avenue you will find the Mainstay Inn, one of the most lavish in the city. Just off the intersection of Columbia Avenue and Guerney Street is the Gingerbread House, an 1869 Victorian cottage with a breezy front porch.

The best way to see it all is to make a loop. From Columbia, go 2 blocks and turn right on Howard Street. Turn left on Stockton Avenue, where you are able to see several more Victorian inns.

A favorite with visitors to Cape May is the Victorian Lace Inn, which has spacious rooms and ocean views. Not all of the Victorian homes have been converted into bed & breakfast accommodations; it only seems that way!

On Stockton Avenue, go 2 blocks to Queen Street and turn right. This will take you back to Beach Avenue, where you turn right to complete the loop.

The Lewes–Cape May Ferry (*photo by Orlando V. Wootten*)

From Beach Avenue, go 5 blocks to Ocean Street and continue 3 blocks to Washington Street. You are now in the mall area; it is best to lock your bike in a rack and continue on foot. As you come up Ocean Street, the mall will be on your left.

Sample some ice cream from one of several sweet shops, find a bench, and watch the parade of vacationers pass by.

No visit to Washington Street is complete without a visit to the old Victorian fire station and museum, which is located 1 block east from the mall at the corner of Washington and Franklin Streets. The fire station looks as it did at the turn of the century. Climb upstairs to the small loft and you will be able to see how the firemen slid down the pole to the awaiting engine when fires broke out in Cape May.

If time permits, you will want to visit the Emlen Physick House and Estate, which is located 1 mile from the mall at 1048 Washington Street in the northeast section of Cape May. Built in 1881, this mansion contains elaborate chimneys, dormers, and trim. It is now a Victorian museum containing a fascinating collection of Victorian furniture, clothing, toys, tools, and memorabilia.

If you are a day-tripping cyclist who has put in several hours at Cape May, check your watch. Mind the ferry schedule! There is more to see before you leave.

Backtracking out of Cape May from the Washington Street Mall, proceed 1 block north to Lafayette Avenue. Turn left on Lafayette Avenue and after 1 block turn right on Jackson Street. Proceed 1 block to Perry Street and turn left on Perry Street. This will lead you directly out to Sunset Boulevard. Continue straight and head due south for Cape May Point.

It is an easy 20-minute bike ride (3 miles) to the Cape May Light House and Cape May Point, a wildlife sanctuary.

The present lighthouse has stood guard here since 1859. Nearby Lake Lilly, a body of fresh water, attracts thousands of ducks and shore birds. Cape May Point was originally developed in the 1870s by a group of prominent Philadelphia Presbyterians headed by department store tycoon John Wanamaker.

A Note for the Return Ride

Simply retrace your steps back toward Cape May. From Sunset Boulevard, turn left on NJ 607. Continue until you pick up US 9 to the ferry terminal.

Bicycle Repair Services

Shaffers Bike Service (302-645-8713) 351 Hwy. 1 and Red Mill Pond Rd., 4 miles north of Lewes, DE.

Hale Bicycle Company (609-465-3126), 3–5 Mechanic St., Cape May, NJ.

Attractions

The Emlen Physick House, 1048 Washington St., Cape May, NJ is open to the public daily in the summer and on weekends in spring and fall.

The Mid-Atlantic Center for the Arts (609-884-5404), 1048 Washington

St., PO Box 164, Cape May, NJ 08204 sponsors tours of Victorian houses in Cape May from April through December.

Lodging

Alexander's Inn (609-884-2555), 653 Washington St., Cape May, NJ 08204. 4 rooms, private baths.

Carroll Villa (609-884-9619), Jackson St., Cape May, NJ 08204. 26 rooms, 11 with private bath.

The Chalfonte (609-884-8409), PO Box 475, Cape May, NJ 08204. This rambling Victorian inn is located on the corner of Howard Street and Sewell Avenue and is 2 blocks from the beach. Each April when the hotel reopens guests are invited to stay gratis in exchange for wallpapering, painting, carpentry, or whatever. 103 rooms, 11 with private bath.

The Gingerbread House (609-884-0211), 28 Gurney St., Cape May, NJ 08204.

The Mainstay (609-884-8690), 635 Columbia Ave., Cape May, NJ 08204. 13 rooms, 9 with private bath.

Note: Although Cape May has dozens of Victorian inns as well as hotels and motels, it can be difficult to get weekend reservations in the summer. The Cape May Reservation Service represents the vast majority of inns, hotels, and motels in town. Telephone 1-800-729-7778.

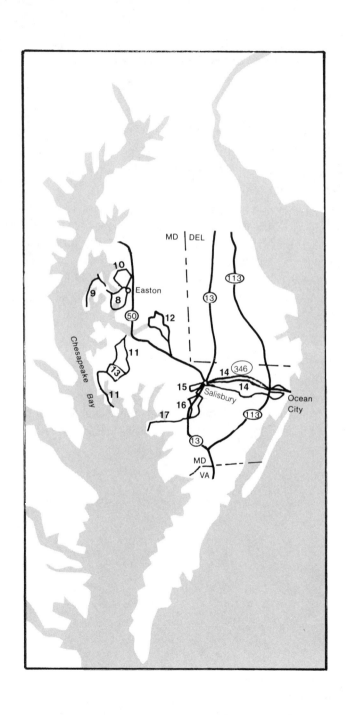

THE MID–CHESAPEAKE BAY
REGION

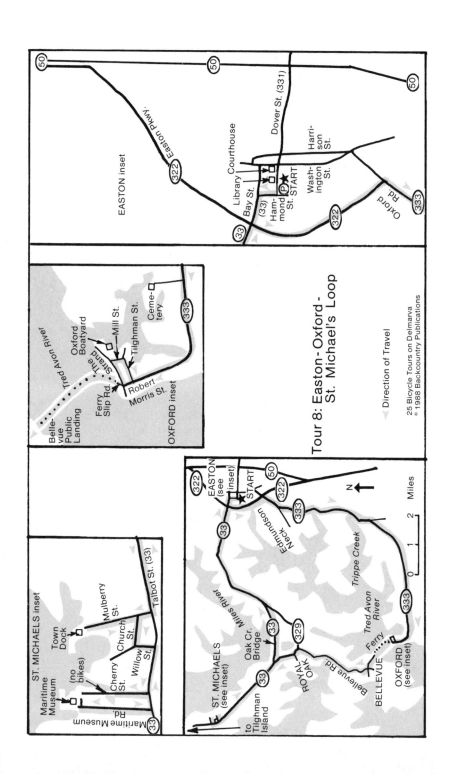

ST. MICHAELS inset

Maritime Museum
(no bikes)
Town Dock
Mulberry St.
Cherry St.
Church St.
Willow St.
Talbot St. (33)
Maritime Museum Rd.
33

OXFORD inset

Bellevue Public Landing
Tred Avon River
Oxford Boatyard
The Strand
Mill St.
Tilghman St.
Ferry Slip Rd.
Robert Morris St.
Cemetery
333

EASTON inset

50
50
50
Easton Pkwy.
322
333
Oxford Rd.
Dover St. (331)
Harrison St.
Washington St.
Library
Courthouse
Bay St.
(33)
Hammond St.
P
START
33
322

Tour 8: Easton - Oxford - St. Michael's Loop

▶ Direction of Travel

25 Bicycle Tours on Delmarva
© 1988 Backcountry Publications

N

Miles
0   1   2

322
EASTON (see inset)
START
50
322
333
33
Edmundson Neck
Trippe Creek
Miles River
Oak Cr. Bridge
33
329
ROYAL OAK
Bellevue Rd.
Tred Avon River
Ferry
BELLEVUE
OXFORD (see inset)
333
ST. MICHAELS (see inset)
33
P
to Tilghman Island

8
Easton–Oxford–St. Michaels Loop

Distance: 31 miles
Terrain: Flat countryside, one ferry crossing
Location: Talbot County, Maryland
Special features: Easton, Oxford, Oxford-Bellevue Ferry, Royal Oak, St.
Michaels, Chesapeake Bay Maritime Museum

This is the kind of trip that both novice and experienced cyclists dream about. The countryside is lovely at any time of year. There are exquisite country towns and villages dating from before the founding of our republic. The roads are of good quality and have well-marked bike lanes. Thus, you should not be surprised to discover that this is probably the most popular bicycle trip in Chesapeake Bay country. On all my routes on the Delmarva Peninsula, this is the only tour where I have seen more than seven cyclists at any one time.

Like all trips to attractive historic areas, this one has its drawbacks. Highway 33, the main route connecting St. Michaels and Easton, has heavy traffic on the weekends. Stick well to the side of the road and use caution in crossing the bridge at Oak Creek just before St. Michaels. On the weekends, St. Michaels is crowded, and you'll probably have a much better time if you travel midweek during the summer. Also, this part of the Eastern Shore is stunning in September and October.

Easton is a busy little Eastern Shore town, and its streets can sometimes be a puzzle for the tourist. There are two easy ways to enter Easton. If you are arriving from US 50 from the north, turn right 1 mile north of Easton on MD 322. Follow this road for 3 miles to the intersection of MD 322 and MD 33. Turn left on Bay Street. After 0.3 mile, turn right on Hammond Street. After 1 block, turn left on Dover Street. This will put you at one of the few free municipal parking lots in Easton. Parking is

Chesapeake Bay Maritime Museum in St. Michaels

heavily metered, and the meter maids are diligent in giving tickets to parking violators; hence the elaborate directions in getting you to this lot.

If you are coming to Easton on US 50 from the south, turn left at the intersection of US 50 and MD 331 onto Dover Street. Follow Dover Street 2 miles to the municipal parking lot. Another advantage in starting from this area is that it is across the street from the Talbot County Library, where the 18th-century-styled Maryland Room is well worth a visit.

While some old Eastern Shore towns seem content to bask in the vanished glories of the past, Easton is as vigorous, proud, and pretty as it was in the 18th century. Before the American Revolution, Easton was the capital of the Eastern Shore; the difficulties of travel necessitated having two Maryland capitals, one at Annapolis, the other on the Eastern Shore. Today Easton wears its mantle easily as the colonial capital, although around the downtown courthouse there are more buildings from the Victorian era than the colonial period.

The Court House Square area is the showpiece of Easton, and there are many elegant shops to browse in. The restaurants in the area are nice though expensive. At the Court House you will see a memorial to the Confederate veterans of Talbot County who fought in the Civil War. As many more Talbot Countians fought for the North than the South, this memorial has been a sore point with many local residents over the years. Old disputes die hard on the Eastern Shore!

While you enjoy exploring Easton, watch out for the one-way streets. At the corner of Dover and Harrison Streets is the famous Tidewater Inn, one of the truly great hostelries of the Eastern Shore. In the inn's restaurant, waiters still wear tuxedoes, and the fare is strictly of the Chesapeake region. If you come to Easton during goose hunting season, the lobby of the Tidewater Inn will be alive with the yapping of retrievers, since hunters can keep their dogs in their rooms.

Before leaving Easton on the first leg of your journey, be sure to visit the Talbot Historical Society Museum at 29 South Washington Street. Afterwards, continue on South Washington 1 mile to the Third Haven Quaker Meeting House. This clapboard structure was built between 1682 and 1684 and is one of the oldest wooden frame houses of worship in the United States. During the colonial period, Easton had a significant population of Quakers. After spending a few hours in Easton, prepare to head south to Oxford. The open road awaits you.

Talbot County has always been wealthy. In the colonial period, it was the heart of the Chesapeake's tobacco empire, and in the antebellum period it was the grain capital of the region. Slavery and the plantation style of life died hard here, and many of the fine old manor houses are just visible from the road. Frederick A. Douglass, the famous black orator and abolitionist of the Civil War era, fled from a plantation in Talbot County.

Today, Talbot County has become a sailing capital and enclave of some of the richest families in America. The grand manor houses that enabled the old planter class to live and entertain with grace are now owned by corporate chieftains. Talbot has more millionaires per square mile than any other county in Maryland. Small wonder that the county is nicknamed the Gold Coast.

Directions for the Ride

0.0 We begin our journey to Oxford from the municipal parking lot on Dover Street in Easton. From the lot, turn left on Dover Street. At the stop sign turn right on Hammond Street.

0.2 Turn left at the stop sign onto Bay Street.

0.5 At the traffic light turn left on MD 322 for Oxford.

You will soon be on Edmundson Neck. Narrow pieces of land that jut out into creeks or rivers, these necks are high and well drained with access to boat moorings, making them logical places for the planters to build their mansions.

1.9   *Turn right on MD 333 south. This is the Oxford road.*

3.9   *Peach Blossom Creek Bridge provides a lovely vista of yachts anchored in the creek.*

5.4   *Trippe Creek Bridge.*

10.6 *Enter Oxford.*

Just before you pass into the town limits of Oxford, the Oxford cemetery will be on your right. It is the burying ground of the Tilghman family and other members of the colonial aristocracy that ruled Talbot County in the 18th and 19th centuries.

Oxford sits comfortably on a peninsula bordered by the Tred Avon and Choptank Rivers. During the colonial period, Oxford flourished as a tobacco and shipping center. Its fortunes were linked with the economic exploits of Robert Morris Sr., who came to Oxford in 1738 as the agent of the Liverpool merchant firm of Foster Cunliffe. Morris made a fortune in tobacco, lumber, and fur for his factors in Liverpool and himself as well. His son, Robert Morris Jr., moved to Philadelphia and played an important role in helping to finance the American Revolution. Understandably, Oxford's main thoroughfare is named Robert Morris Street.

11.5 *Robert Morris Inn.*

Once the residence of Robert Morris, the inn dates from 1774 and has been tastefully restored. The inn overlooks the Tred Avon River and is a stone's throw from the slips of the Oxford-Bellevue Ferry.

From the Robert Morris Inn, continue right onto the Strand.

This lovely road goes right alongside the Tred Avon River, and there are plenty of boats in the harbor to capture your attention.

11.8 *Turn right on Mill Street. This will take you past the Oxford Boat Yard and Marina. At the stop sign turn right on Tilghman Street.*

12.1 *Turn right on Robert Morris Street and return to the Robert Morris Inn and prepare to take the ferry.*

You may wish to check out the Oxford Mews Bike Boutique that is just up from Clark's Bed and Breakfast Inn at 110 Robert Morris Street. (To get to the boutique and bed & breakfast, turn left at Tilghman Street.)

12.2 *Oxford-Bellevue Ferry.*

My wife, Ruth Ellen, and I crossed the Tred Avon River on a sunny September day. The sky was crystal blue, and several large Chesapeake sailboats were coming into port. I gladly paid the boatswain the $1.50 per person toll for a truly majestic river crossing.

12.5 *After cycling down the pier from the ferry slip, you will enter Bellevue.*

Once a poor town of cannery and seafood-house workers, Bellevue is becoming gentrified with vacation estates.

13.0 *Turn right on Bellevue Road. A road sign points to St. Michaels.*

15.9 *After the village of Royal Oak, turn left on MD 329.*

Royal Oak boasts a thriving antiques emporium and a country store. It is also the home of the Pasadena, a charming country hotel on a tributary of the Miles River. It is a favorite hideaway for Maryland artists and writers.

16.9 *At the stop sign you will be at the junction of MD 329 and MD 33. Turn left on MD 33 West.*

19.5 *Enter St. Michaels.*

Traffic in St. Michaels on the weekends can be heavy. As you proceed down Talbot Street into the village, be careful. Often, gawking tourists driving through town are unmindful of pedestrians.

Although a certain amount of tourist pollution has affected St. Michaels, it is still one of the most charming villages on the Eastern Shore. The town harbor and wharves are still important entrepôts for Chesapeake watermen, and at various times during the day you can watch them unloading their catches of crabs and oysters on the town dock. Many of the homes in St. Michaels date from the colonial period. To cycle through St. Michaels is to cycle through history. St. Michaels is the oldest town in Talbot County and was a trading center as early as the 1630s.

St. Michaels played an important role in the War of 1812. Here were equipped many of the privateers that preyed upon British oceangoing commerce. According to local history, the shipyards of St. Michaels constructed vessels that were responsible for the capture or destruction of over 500 British merchant ships. So great a threat was St. Michaels that the British attacked the town on August 9, 1813. The town imposed a blackout, and its shrewd citizens placed lanterns in the trees to misdirect the artillery barrage, thus fooling the British. Only one house was struck, and it is known today as the Cannonball House.

In the 1960s, St. Michaels awoke from the somnolence of rural life when the Chesapeake Bay Maritime Museum was founded in the town. The museum was dedicated to the lore and history of the Chesapeake, and its attractive exhibits made it a mecca for bay country visitors. There is much to learn here about the history of the bay and its traditions in boatbuilding, commercial fishing, yachting, and navigation. A favorite attraction is the 100-year-old Chesapeake Bay lighthouse that was dismantled and brought to the museum. From the museum, you will have a lovely vista of the harbor and the Miles River; and on a bright fall day there may be dozens of sailing craft flying before the wind on the river.

19.9 **To explore the town of St. Michaels, turn right on Mulberry Street when you enter the village.**

This will get you away from the Talbot Street traffic and down to the town dock. At the dock, spend some time watching the watermen or talking to the owners of expensive powerboats that are moored here. Mulberry Street is one of the prettiest in St. Michaels. At 200 Mulberry Street is the Cannonball House.

20.3 **Retrace your way back up Mulberry Street. Turn right on Church Street and take a quick left on Willow Street. This will take you back to Talbot Street, the main thoroughfare, where you turn right.**

20.5 **Turn right on Cherry Street.**

There are many old Chesapeake Bay mariner's homes here for you to see. Beware of the signs at the footbridge to the Chesapeake Bay Maritime Museum that say "No Bikes!"

To get to the museum, go back out Cherry Street. Turn right on Talbot Street and then right again on Maritime Museum Road.

There is a large parking lot for the museum at the end of this lane, and you can park your bike here and visit the museum grounds.

A Note on the Return Ride

When you have fully savored St. Michaels, retrace your route on Talbot Street out of town to MD 33 East. (If you continue through St. Michaels on MD 33 West, you will go to Tilghman Island.)

23.9 *At the junction of MD 33 and MD 329 East, stay on MD 33 for Easton. MD 329 takes you back to the ferry and Oxford.*

24.5 *Oak Creek Bridge. Be careful of traffic.*

30.4 *Junction and traffic light of MD 33 and MD 322. Continue straight through the light on MD 33 into Easton.*

30.7 *MD 33 becomes Bay Street. Turn right on Hammond Street.*

30.9 *Turn left on Dover Street into the municipal parking lot.*

31.0 *Reach the municipal parking lot and the end of your journey.*

Bicycle Repair Services

Bicycles Unlimited (410-822-8666), US 50 North, Easton, MD.

Oxford Mews Bike Boutique (410-820-8222), 105 S. Morris St., Oxford, MD.

Attractions

Academy of the Arts, 201 South St., Easton, MD. A regional arts center serving the Eastern Shore.

Historical Society Museum, 25 S. Washington St., Easton, MD. Modern museum galleries devoted to 18th- and 19th-century Maryland life. Open Tuesday through Saturday 10–4.

Oxford-Bellevue Ferry, Oxford, MD. Believed to be the oldest "free-running ferry"—one that runs under its own power—in the United States. Operates Monday through Friday 7 AM–9 PM. Reduced schedule after Labor Day.

St. Mary's Square Museum, St. Michaels, MD. The museum, located in the delightful St. Mary's Square, is housed in the old Teetotum Building and contains items significant to the local history of St. Michaels. Open Saturday and Sunday 10–4.

Lodging

Kemp House Inn (410-745-2243), 412 Talbot St., St. Michaels, MD 21663. 7 rooms.

McDaniel House B&B (410-822-3704 or 1-800-787-INNS), 14 N. Aurora St., Easton, MD 21601.

Oxford Inn and Pope's Tavern (410-226-5520), 510 Morris St., Oxford, MD 21654. 11 rooms, private baths.

The Pasadena Inn (410-745-5053), MD 329, Royal Oak, MD 21662.

Robert Morris Inn (410-226-5111), Morris St., Oxford, MD 21654.

Tidewater Inn (410-822-1300), Dover and Harrison Sts., Easton, MD 21601. Expensive.

Victoriana Inn (410-745-3368), 205 Cherry St., St. Michaels, MD 21663.

Note: While there are a number of hotels and inns on this route, they are usually booked in advance during the summer and festivals. For St. Michaels, especially, it pays to use the Maryland Reservation Center. Reach this hotel and inn service by calling 1-800-654-9303.

9

St. Michaels–Tilghman Island

Distance: 34.1 miles
Terrain: Flat countryside
Location: Talbot County, Maryland
Special features: St. Michaels, Tilghman Island, Claiborne

You should consider this tour the second part of your trip around the Oxford–St. Michaels area; if you have a few days, combine this with Tour 8. As you cycle, remember that you are traveling through one of the oldest-settled areas of Maryland, the ancestral domain of the famous Tilghman and Lloyd families. Proud grain farmers, shippers, entrepreneurs, slaveholders, and politicians, the Lloyds and the Tilghmans ruled Talbot County in the 18th and 19th centuries much like the Cabots and Lodges ruled old Boston. This is also the ancestral land of the famous black abolitionist and social reformer Frederick A. Douglass, who escaped in his youth from the slave-owning Lloyds.

The ride west and south on MD 33 from St. Michaels to Tilghman Island is an easy one. The roads are well marked and there is plenty of highway shoulder. In the fall, however, expect to encounter occasional stiff westerly winds that will slow you down considerably. But at least you will have the wind at your back for the return trip!

Once you arrive at Tilghman Island, take time to explore. Tilghman Islanders are not the taciturn sort; they like to talk to strangers about their boats and their seafaring way of life. Plan to take your camera as there are plenty of sailing vessels and Chesapeake work boats to photograph.

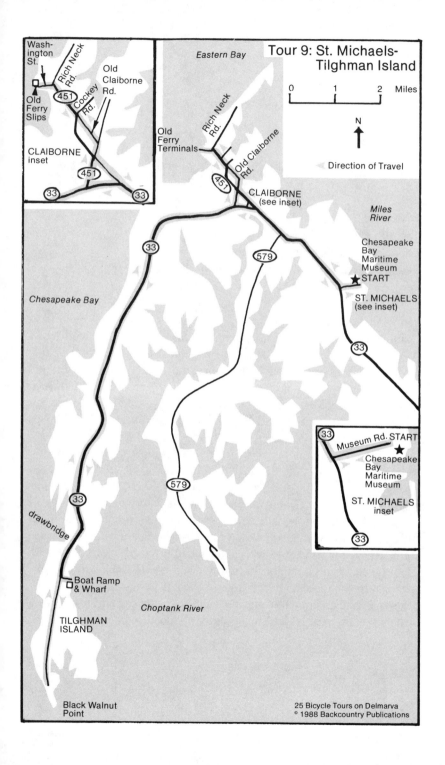

CLAIBORNE inset

Washington St.

Old Ferry Slips

Rich Neck Rd.

Old Claiborne Rd.

Cockey Rd.

451

451

33

33

Eastern Bay

Tour 9: St. Michaels-Tilghman Island

0   1   2   Miles

N

◁ Direction of Travel

Old Ferry Terminals

Rich Neck Rd.

Old Claiborne Rd.

451

CLAIBORNE (see inset)

Miles River

Chesapeake Bay Maritime Museum START

ST. MICHAELS (see inset)

33

579

Chesapeake Bay

33

33

579

579

drawbridge

33

Boat Ramp & Wharf

TILGHMAN ISLAND

Choptank River

33

Museum Rd. START

★

Chesapeake Bay Maritime Museum

ST. MICHAELS inset

33

Black Walnut Point

25 Bicycle Tours on Delmarva
© 1988 Backcountry Publications

Directions for the Ride

0.0 *The trip begins at the parking lot of the Chesapeake Bay Maritime Museum, which is located on Museum Street. There are signs in St. Michaels that point the way to the museum (see Tour 8).*

0.2 *Proceed down Museum Street and turn right on Talbot Street. Talbot Street soon becomes Tilghman Island Road/MD 33.*

0.5 *Perry Cabin.*

Now a fashionable Chesapeake country inn and restaurant, Perry Cabin was built before the American Revolution. Greatly expanded in the 19th century, it was named in honor of Commodore Oliver H. Perry, the victorious American naval commander on Lake Erie during the War of 1812. The inn is open to the public, so you may cycle onto the grounds. Park your bike and walk around to the water side of the inn, where you will have an excellent view of the Miles River.

3.4 *Junction of MD 33 and MD 451. Bear left on MD 33.*

5.0 *Wades Point Inn, a local bed & breakfast establishment, is on your right.*

7.5 *On your right you will be able to see the bay across the cornfields.*

12.9 *Drawbridge at Tilghman Island.*

I think this is one of the prettiest spots in Talbot County because it offers a lovely vista of boats of all sizes passing through the Tilghman Island Straits en route to either the bay or the Choptank River.

On your right just before the bridge is the Bay Hundred Restaurant. In summer, order a refreshing drink and sit out on the veranda and watch the boats pass by. This restaurant is owned by a young couple who are happy to host long-distance cyclists.

After resting, cross the bridge onto Tilghman Island.

You'll find that this little community of fishermen and crabbers is a fairly busy spot. The place is cluttered with piles of wire crab pots and molting sheds for softshelled crabs.

13.4 Turn left onto the boat ramp and wharf.

Much like Deal Island (see Tour 17), Tilghman Island is home port to a diminishing number of Chesapeake Bay skipjacks. These proud sailing vessels continue to dredge the bay for oysters, often in the foulest of winter weather. The skipjacks, which are over 100 years old and made of wood, have a grace lacking in modern craft. On my last visit by bike to Tilghman Island seven skipjacks were moored here. Among the prettiest of these was the famous skipjack *Hilda Willing*, owned by Captain Pete Switzer of Tilghman. While at the wharf, you may have a chance to see a boat being rebuilt or overhauled by local shipwrights.

After leaving the wharf, turn left on MD 33 and continue south on Tilghman Island.

13.6 Harrison's Chesapeake House will be on your left.

Park your bike in the parking lot and walk around this resort's grounds. From here you will have an excellent view of the mouth of the Choptank River. On a clear day you will be able to see Taylors Island in Dorchester County. The inn is a favorite with sportfishers and duck hunters.

15.0 St. John's Methodist Church will be on your right.

Shipwrights rebuild a skipjack on Tilghman Island.

16.1 *Black Walnut Point and Coast Guard Station.*

You are at the end of the island. From the parking lot you have a good view of Chesapeake Bay, and on a clear day you can see Calvert County on the western shore.

A Note for the Return Ride

Retrace your route back to the Tilghman Island Bridge and proceed east on MD 33.

28.0 *Turn left on MD 451 to Claiborne.*

A side trip to this village will help to break the monotony of the return ride.

28.5 *Turn left on Old Claiborne Road.*

29.1 *At the intersection of Old Claiborne Road and Cockey Road, turn left then quickly right on MD 451 and enter Claiborne.*

Named for William Claiborne, the English adventurer who established a trading post on Kent Island in the 17th century (see Tour 1), the town of Claiborne is today a sleepy Chesapeake hamlet. Before the opening of the Chesapeake Bay Bridge, however, it was an important auto ferry terminal for connections between Talbot County and Kent Island.

One mile outside of Claiborne on Rich Neck Road is Rich Neck Manor, the ancestral seat of the Tilghman family. Matthew Tilghman rode from this plantation to Philadelphia to take his position in the Continental Congress during the American Revolution.

29.6 *A right turn will take you up Rich Neck Road to the Tilghman plantation. A left turn on Rich Neck Road will take you to the old ferry slips.*

29.8 *At the old ferry slips you can see Kent Island straight ahead across the water. The slips are a good place to have a picnic or swim. After you have relaxed a bit, pedal back on Rich Neck Road and turn right on MD 451.*

31.6 *At the intersection of MD 451 and MD 33, turn left on MD 33.*

33.9 Return to St. Michaels. Turn left on Museum Street.

34.1 Reach the museum parking lot and the end of your loop.

Bicycle Repair Services

Oxford Mews Bike Boutique (410-820-8222), 105 S. Morris St., Oxford, MD.

Lodging

Black Walnut Point Inn (410-886-2452), Tilghman, MD 21671. 7 rooms, private baths.

Chesapeake Wood Duck Inn (1-800-956-2070), Gibsontown Rd., Tilghman, MD 21671. 6 rooms, private baths.

Harrison's Chesapeake House (410-886-2123), 5831 Main St., Tilghman, MD 21671.

Lazyjack Inn (410-886-2215), 5907 Tilghman Island Rd., Tilghman Island, MD 21676.

10
Easton–Miles River Loop

Distance: 17.2 miles
Terrain: Flat to gently rolling
Location: Talbot County, Maryland
Special features: Easton, Miles River, Unionville

This trip complements Tours 8 and 9 and is designed for either the novice or experienced cyclist who wishes to spend a morning or afternoon cycling out of Easton through the countryside of Talbot County. This tour is a perfect Sunday outing, especially after you have had one of those superb brunches at either the Peach Blossom Restaurant or the Tidewater Inn and want to aid your digestion with some low-key cycling.

In the fall you can hardly go more than a mile out of Easton before you begin to hear the excited honking of thousands of Canada geese. The fields are full of them, especially on misty mornings. At the opening of goose hunting season, which is usually around the second week of November, over 20,000 people flock to Easton to attend the annual Waterfowl Festival, a 3-day show that brings in some of the best waterfowl artists and bird carvers in America to display and sell their work. (For further information on the festival call 410-822-4567.) If you plan to cycle in the Easton area during the Waterfowl Festival, book a hotel room well in advance.

Directions for the Ride

0.0 As in our other loop out of Easton, this tour begins at the municipal parking lot on Dover Street. (See Tour 8 for directions to the parking lot.) Go left on Dover Street out of the lot.

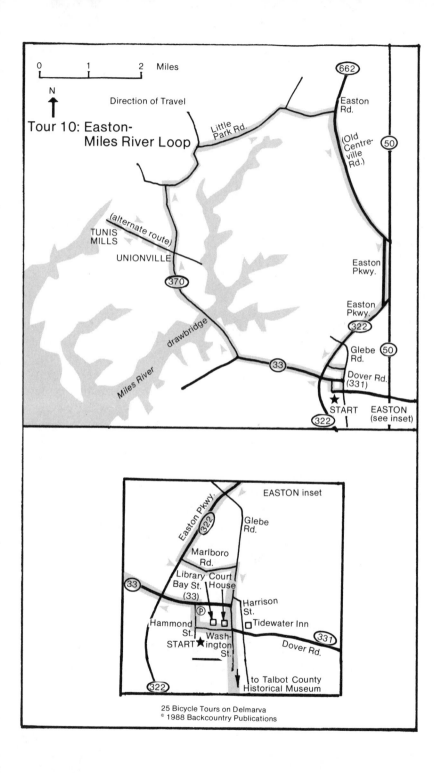

Tour 10: Easton–
Miles River Loop

0   1   2   Miles

N

Direction of Travel

Little Park Rd.

662

Easton Rd.

(Old Centre-ville Rd.)

50

TUNIS MILLS

(alternate route)

UNIONVILLE

370

Easton Pkwy.

Easton Pkwy.

322

drawbridge

Glebe Rd.

50

Miles River

33

Dover Rd. (331)

START

322

EASTON (see inset)

Easton Pkwy.

322

EASTON inset

Glebe Rd.

Marlboro Rd.

Library Court House

33

Bay St. (33)

Harrison St.

P

Tidewater Inn

Hammond St.

331

Dover Rd.

Wash-ington St.

START

to Talbot County Historical Museum

322

25 Bicycle Tours on Delmarva
© 1988 Backcountry Publications

0.1   *Turn right on Hammond Street.*

0.2   *Turn left on Bay Street and proceed to the traffic light.*

0.5   *Cross MD 322 and proceed west on MD 33/St. Michaels–Tilghman Island Road.*

2.3   *Turn right on MD 370. Follow the signs for Tunis Mills and Unionville.*

3.0   *Within 0.5 mile of each other are two famous Eastern Shore manor houses, Rest and the Anchorage.*

During the Civil War, the colorful and prominent Lloyd sisters were the mistresses of each plantation. Unfortunately, Sarah Lloyd Lowndes's husband was a Union naval officer, and the Anchorage was in Federal territory, while Ann Lloyd Buchanan's husband was a Confederate admiral, and Rest was a Dixie stronghold. During the Civil War, Admiral Franklin Buchanan commanded the iron-clad battleship *Virginia* at the Battle of Hampton Roads. He was wounded the day before his ship's celebrated encounter with the USS *Monitor.*

3.1   *When you cross the Miles River Drawbridge, you will have a scenic view of the river and its boat and yacht traffic.*

3.4   *The Anchorage plantation.*

On your right, close to the shoreline, you will see the ruins of St. John's Protestant Episcopal Church. Built in 1839, this chapel served wealthy Miles River gentry who wished to avoid the lengthy trip to church in St. Michaels. You can still see the low, crenellated tower; its crumbling walls provide a worthy setting for a Sir Walter Scott novel.

4.6   *Enter Unionville.*

This historically black village traces its roots to the Civil War era. St. Stephen's African Methodist Episcopal Church will be on your right.

4.9   *Reach the Tunis Mills cutoff. You can turn left and enter the sleepy village or Tunis Mills or else continue straight ahead on Unionville Road. (If you go to Tunis Mills, you will have to come back the same way.)*

6.2 At the stop sign the road comes to a T. Turn right and follow the sign that says "To Route 50."

7.4 The road forks here. Take the right fork and proceed on Little Park Road.

You will quickly come upon a scenic tidewater creek on your right.

Note: *Little Park Road becomes Sharp Road.*

10.4 The road again comes to a T. Turn right at the stop sign onto Easton Road (also called the Old Centreville Road/MD 662). Prepare to climb a hill, which may come as a surprise after miles of flat terrain.

13.4 Continue on Easton/Old Centreville Road. Shortly you will see US 50 on your left, which runs parallel to Easton Road. Continue straight at the stop sign for Easton Municipal Airport.

14.8 At the intersection of Easton Road/MD 662 and Easton Parkway, turn right onto Easton Parkway. Use caution on Easton Parkway as the traffic is brisk at times.

15.4 The Black and Decker power tool plant will be on your right.

15.6 At the traffic light, continue straight on Easton Parkway.

16.2 Turn left on Marlborough Road. Tred Avon Square Shopping Center will be on your right. There is no traffic light here, so use caution in making a left-hand turn.

16.6 Turn right on Glebe Road.

16.9 Glebe Road becomes Washington Street. Continue on Washington Street into downtown Easton.

17.1 At the Talbot County Court House turn right on Dover Street.

17.2 Reach the municipal parking lot and the end of your loop.

Bicycle Repair Services

None on this route.

Ruins of St. John's Episcopal Church on the Miles River

Attractions

Third Haven Friends Meeting House, 405 S. Washington St., Easton, MD. A famous, 1682 Quaker meetinghouse. William Penn preached here; Lord Baltimore attended services. Open daily 9–5.

Lodging

Ashby 1663 B&B (410-822-4235), 27448 Goldsborough Rd., Easton, MD 21601. 9 rooms, private baths.

Econo Lodge (410-822-5555), US 50, Easton, MD 21601.

Gross' Coate 1658 (410-819-0802), 11300 Gross' Coate Rd., Easton, MD 21601. 6 rooms, private baths.

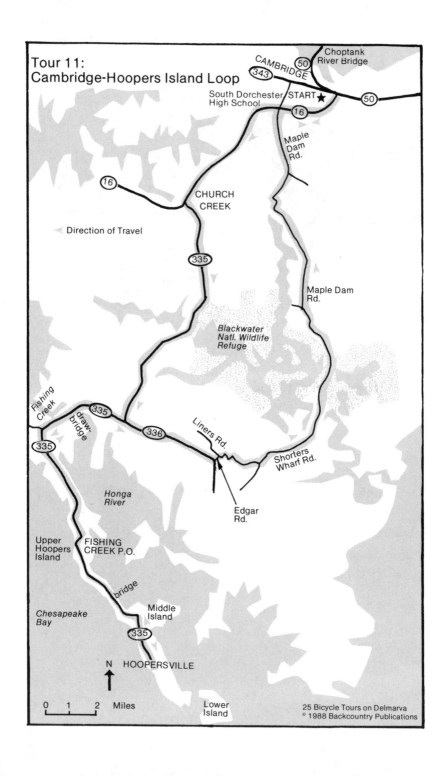

Tour 11:
Cambridge-Hoopers Island Loop

Choptank
River Bridge

CAMBRIDGE
50
343

South Dorchester
High School

START ★

50

16

Maple
Dam
Rd.

16

CHURCH
CREEK

Direction of Travel

335

Maple Dam
Rd.

Blackwater
Natl. Wildlife
Refuge

Fishing
Creek

draw-bridge

335

336

Liners Rd.

Shorters
Wharf Rd.

335

Honga
River

Edgar
Rd.

Upper
Hoopers
Island

FISHING
CREEK P.O.

bridge

Chesapeake
Bay

Middle
Island

335

N

HOOPERSVILLE

0   1   2   Miles

Lower
Island

25 Bicycle Tours on Delmarva
© 1988 Backcountry Publications

11

Cambridge–Hoopers Island Loop

Distance: *65.7 miles*
Terrain: *Flat farmland giving way to marsh*
Location: *Dorchester County, Maryland*
Special features: *Church Creek, Hoopers Island, Blackwater Marsh*

The trip to Hoopers Island provides an excellent opportunity to see a large portion of Dorchester County, Maryland, and indeed Dorchester is Maryland's largest county. (You can do this tour in conjunction with Tour 13 if you like.) This is tidewater country at its best, and the marshes and small farm communities are tied together through the cycle of nature. The cornfields attract thousands of Canada geese from the marsh. On early fall mornings the fields are virtually black with these honkers. Thus, Dorchester is a waterfowl hunter's paradise, and many farmers supplement their incomes by leasing duck and goose blinds on their property.

South of Church Creek, the Dorchester landscape turns wild and swampy as you pass through the western corner of Blackwater Wildfowl Refuge. Soon the marsh gives way to the Honga River and you approach Hoopers Island, a prosperous community of watermen and boatbuilders. Down on the Honga River, the city of Cambridge seems very far away indeed.

Like all marsh routes discussed in this book, avoid this one in summer because of the insects. The best time to take this route is in the fall, when the marsh begins to turn golden brown and thousands of migratory ducks and geese make Dorchester a birdwatcher's delight. On this tour, a pair of binoculars will come in handy. It is best to begin this loop at dawn, as the tour requires a full day of cycling.

The Methodist Church on Hoopers Island

Directions for the Ride

0.0   The trip begins at South Dorchester High School, which is located just south of Cambridge. The school is located at the intersection of MD 16 and MD 343. It is easy to find, and on the weekend you can park your car in the school lot. On weekdays, park on one of the local side streets. By starting at South Dorchester High School, you can avoid the traffic congestion and construction on US 50. From Cambridge, take US 50 south and turn right onto MD 16 and continue for 1.5 miles.

3.8   Enter Church Creek.

This old community developed around Trinity Church in the 1690s. For years, oystering and tomato canneries supported the town, but these days most of the villagers work in Cambridge. Trinity Church itself was built in 1675 and is the oldest church in the United States still in active use. It was restored in the 1960s. (You'll find the church 1 mile outside the village on MD 16.)

4.8 *Turn left at the Church Creek Post Office onto MD 335.*

Now you will be traveling through the Kentuck Swamp and Blackwater Refuge. It is difficult to determine whether Somerset County or Dorchester County marshes are more beautiful. Aubrey Bodine, the famous Maryland photographer, had a definite opinion, however, naming the south Dorchester marsh the most beautiful spot in Maryland. Here you will see vast waving fields of marsh grass and patches of sparkling water that reflect a bright autumn sky. You will want to stop often to gaze at the snow geese and marsh gulls.

14.8 *Come to a crossroads. At the junction of MD 335 and MD 336, turn right on MD 335 toward Hoopers Island.*

18.1 *In the midst of this very Protestant countryside, you suddenly come upon Tubman Chapel.*

This 18th-century Roman Catholic church was founded by the Tubman family and other Catholics who migrated to Dorchester across the bay from St. Mary's County in the late 17th century. This was the site of the first Catholic community in Dorchester County, and today the nearby St. Mary's Star of the Sea ministers to the needs of the small group of Catholics who live here.

21.3 *An old wooden drawbridge crosses Fishing Creek to Upper Hoopers Island.*

Hoopers Island is actually a chain of three islands that run parallel to the mainland of Dorchester County. The Honga River estuary will be on your left as you head south. In winter the waters and marshes of the Honga are reported to contain the largest concentrations of wild ducks and geese in the United States.

Originally the island was a farming community, but the relentless encroachment of the marsh and the Chesapeake Bay forced the islanders to turn to the water for a living. Even today you can see areas of land, now salt marsh, that were marked by fence posts for fields and pasture.

22.5 *Fishing Creek Post Office is the main area of settlement on Hoopers Island.*

The houses of the village seem to merge with water; backyards face the Chesapeake Bay and front yards face the Honga. Several crab houses operate here, and the village is famed for its steamed crabs. Try lunch at Old Salty's, the only restaurant on the island.

25.1 Cross the causeway and bridge to the middle island.

The bridge is new, and from its crest you can see all of Hoopers Island. In bad weather the waves from the Chesapeake crash across the causeway.

29.5 Hoopersville and Rippons Seafood Company.

Hoopersville is strictly a watermen's hamlet, and you can see soft-shelled crab sheds where the fishermen deposit their catch of crabs and fish. It is a sparse though tightly knit community.

30.0 Dead end of Hoopers Island.

The third island has been totally engulfed by marsh. On your left is a privately owned goose hunting club that is replete with its own air-conditioned wine cellar and party rooms.

A Note for the Return Ride

Leave the island and go back out on MD 335.

45.2 Turn right on MD 336.

49.0 Turn left on Edgar Road.

49.3 Turn right at the stop sign onto Liners Road. You will encounter 1 mile of dirt road as you pass through the swamp.

51.0 Turn left onto Maple Dam Road.

This is a great stretch of highway in autumn as it takes you across the very center of Blackwater Marsh.

65.7 Approach the entrance of South Dorchester High School and the end of the journey.

Bicycle Repair Services

Bike Shop (410-228-7554 or 1-800-660-5860), 523 Race St., Cambridge, MD.

Attractions

Annie Oakley House, 28 Bellevue Ave., Cambridge, MD. This private home was designed and built in 1912 by Wild West sharpshooter Annie Oakley when she and her husband retired to Cambridge.

Dorchester Arts Center (410-228-7782), 120 High St., Cambridge, MD. Three galleries display local paintings, sculptures, crafts, and photographs. Open Monday through Friday 10–2.

Dorchester Heritage Museum (410-228-1899), Horn Point Rd., Cambridge, MD. Highlights local and maritime heritage. Open daily, April 15 through October 30, 1–4:30; open Saturday and Sunday 1–4:30 year-round.

Hoopers Island comprises three islands: Upper, Middle, and Lower. Some properties here have the earliest colonial land grants in Dorchester County—issued in 1659. Early settlers came from St. Mary's across the bay. Supposedly, the island was bought from Native Americans in exchange for blankets.

Lodging

Econo Lodge (410-221-0800), US 50, Cambridge, MD 21613.

Commodore's Cottage (410-228-6938), Brannock Maritime Museum, 210 Talbot St., Cambridge, MD 21613. Spend the night in a Chesapeake Colonial cottage!

Glasgow Inn (410-228-0575), 1500 Hambrooks Blvd., Cambridge, MD 21613. 7 rooms, private baths.

Oakley House (410-228-7020), 906 Locust St., Cambridge, MD 21613. 3 rooms. (This is not the Annie Oakley House!)

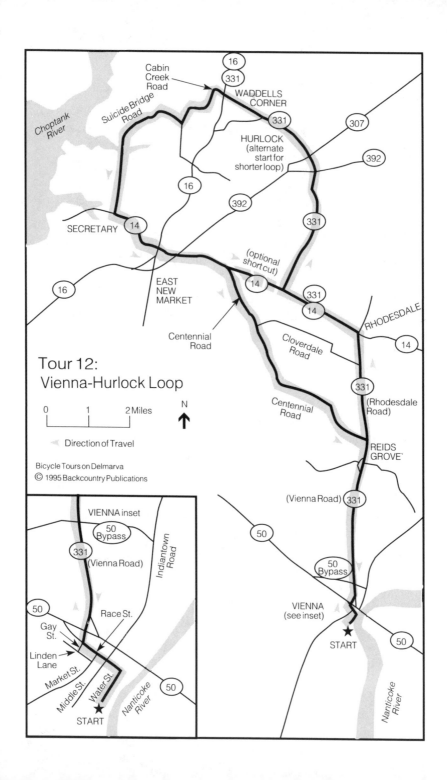

Cabin
Creek
Road

16
331

WADDELLS
CORNER

331

307

HURLOCK
(alternate
start for
shorter loop)

392

16

392

331

331

14

SECRETARY

14

EAST
NEW
MARKET

(optional
short cut)

14

331

14

RHODESDALE

Cloverdale
Road

14

Centennial
Road

331

(Rhodesdale
Road)

Tour 12:
Vienna-Hurlock Loop

0   1   2 Miles

N

Direction of Travel

Bicycle Tours on Delmarva
© 1995 Backcountry Publications

Centennial
Road

REIDS
GROVE

(Vienna Road) 331

50

50
Bypass

VIENNA inset

50
Bypass

331
(Vienna Road)

VIENNA
(see inset)

Indiantown
Road

50

Race St.

50

Gay
St.

Linden
Lane

Market St.

Middle St.

Water St.

START

Nanticoke
River

50

START

Nanticoke
River

Choptank
River

Suicide Bridge
Road

12
Vienna-Hurlock Loop

Distance: *33 miles*
Terrain: *Flat to rolling farmland*
Location: *Dorchester County, Maryland*
Special features: *Vienna, Hurlock, East New Market*

This trip lets you explore the northern half of Dorchester County. It follows the old colonial stage route that connected Vienna and Easton, Maryland, with the communities of Caroline County. The area was once a major cannery center, though—sad to say—only one tomato cannery remains along this route.

Your tour begins in Vienna, a pleasant village situated on the banks of the Nanticoke River. For many years, Vienna was a "gas and go" strip for holiday drivers en route to the beaches of Ocean City. Then the new bridge across the Nanticoke River on US 50 bypassed the town, and Vienna reverted to its former status as a pleasant rural community. Settled as early as 1706, Vienna was the site of the original Nanticoke Indian Reservation designated by Lord Baltimore in Dorchester County in the late 17th century. During the Revolution, pirates operated out of Vienna; during the Civil War, Vienna's merchants outfitted Confederate blockade runners with supplies for the Chesapeake region.

Directions for the Ride

0.0 *Park your car at the end of Water Street near the Nanticoke Manor Bed and Breakfast Inn. Proceed down Water Street along the Nanticoke River, to your right.*

Water Street is the site of the old colonial customs house where ships from England docked and paid colonial duties. Two of its old Federal-period houses have been restored as bed & breakfast inns.

0.2 *Turn left on Race Street.*

0.4 *Turn right on Gay Street, which leads to MD 331 North.*

3.6 *Reids Grove, an old cannery center.*

6.7 *At Rhodesdale turn left on MD 331/MD 14.*

8.8 *Turn right on MD 331 North for Hurlock.*

11.3 *Enter Hurlock.*

Once a major cannery center, the town of Hurlock developed as a railway junction in the 19th century. Now it is a rather pleasant country town with general stores and a country restaurant. The Hurlock Free Library, now a branch of the Dorchester County Library, was founded in 1900 and is the oldest public library on Maryland's Eastern Shore.

11.8 *Continue out of Hurlock on MD 331 toward Waddells Corner.*

14.8 *At the Waddells Corner stop sign, continue straight on Cabin Creek Road.*

16.3 *At a stop sign, turn right on Suicide Bridge Road.*

18.1 *Suicide Bridge Restaurant is a countryside oasis.*

Located on the banks of the Choptank River, the restaurant has a wharf and deck that offer a beautiful vista. Well known to cross-country cyclists, this country pub is a good resting point. "Suicide," as it is called locally, is quite lively on weekends.

19.7 *Enter the village of Secretary. Turn left at the stop sign onto Main Street/MD 14.*

20.8 *Enter East New Market. At the intersection of MD 16, marked by a stop sign, continue straight. The volunteer fire department will be on your left. Continue on MD 14 East.*

The oldest town on this route, East New Market was founded in 1800. The town and its immediate vicinity contain a number of classic Federal-period mansions with high, dual chimneys. Just outside of town on MD 14 is Friendship Hall, a private residence, which is one of the best-known plantations of this region.

23.1 *Turn right onto Centennial Road.*

24.3 *Intersection of Centennial Road and Cloverdale Road. Keep right on Centennial.*

28.6 *Turn right onto MD 331.*

32.2 *Enter Vienna.*

33.0 *Turn right onto Water Street and end your tour.*

ALTERNATE ROUTE: Those desiring a smaller loop can begin in Hurlock and complete the Hurlock–Secretary–East New Market route. Instead of turning onto Centennial Road, continue straight on MD 14 until you reach MD 331 North for Hurlock. Take a left and continue on to your starting point.

Bicycle Repair Services

None on this route.

Lodging

Governor's Ordinary (410-376-3530), PO Box 156, Water St., Vienna, MD 21869. 6 rooms, private baths.

Nanticoke Manor House (410-376-3530), PO Box 248, Church and Water Sts., Vienna, MD 21869. 8 rooms, private baths.

North Fork B&B (410-943-4706), 6505 Palmers Rd., Hurlock, MD 21643.

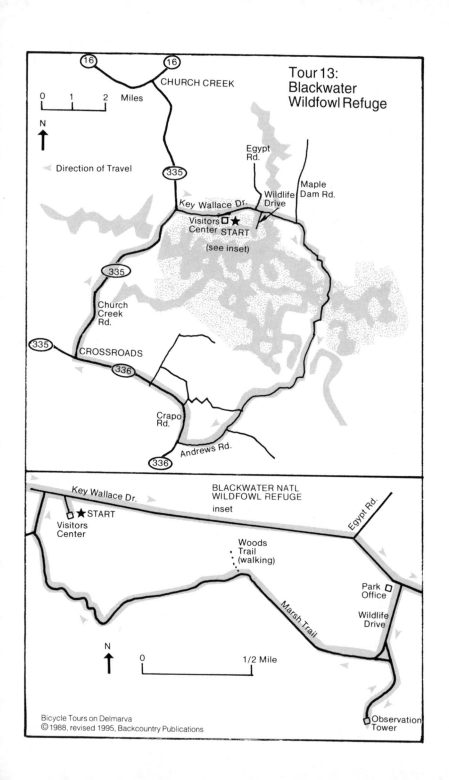

16 16
CHURCH CREEK

Tour 13:
Blackwater
Wildfowl Refuge

0 1 2 Miles

N

Direction of Travel

335

Egypt
Rd.

Maple
Dam Rd.

Key Wallace Dr.

Wildlife
Drive

Visitors
Center START

(see inset)

335

Church
Creek
Rd.

335

CROSSROADS

336

Crapo
Rd.

Andrews Rd.

336

Key Wallace Dr.

BLACKWATER NATL
WILDFOWL REFUGE
inset

Egypt Rd.

START

Visitors
Center

Woods
Trail
(walking)

Park
Office

Marsh Trail

Wildlife
Drive

N

0 1/2 Mile

Observation
Tower

Bicycle Tours on Delmarva
© 1988, revised 1995, Backcountry Publications

13
Blackwater Wildfowl Refuge

Distance: *Short-loop tour: 5.5 miles; long-loop tour: 24 miles*
Terrain: *Swamp and salt marsh*
Location: *Dorchester County, Maryland*
Special features: *Blackwater Wildfowl Refuge*

This tour has the distinction of being this book's shortest ride and one of its most beautiful. As in other rides across the marsh, one rule applies: Do not even think about taking this ride in the summer. The insects are ferocious and the wildfowl do not even begin to arrive from Canada until October. Therefore, schedule this tour for sometime between late September and the end of November.

Blackwater Wildfowl Refuge is located 12 miles south of Cambridge, Maryland. From US 50 by car, take MD 16 south to the village of Church Creek. At Church Creek turn left on MD 335. After 3 miles turn left on Key Wallace Drive and follow the signs to the visitors parking lot at Blackwater Refuge. The visitors center is at the gateway of the refuge and is an excellent starting point for your tour. The center has interesting exhibits about the ecology of the refuge and plenty of tourist information. One caution though: The gate to the parking lot is closed and locked every day at 4 PM.

Since its establishment in 1932 as a refuge for migratory waterfowl, Blackwater has attracted thousands of visitors. Blackwater is one of the chief wintering areas for Canada geese using the Atlantic flyway. At the park's peak in late October or November, there will be about 55,000 geese and 25,000 ducks at the refuge.

If you are serious about combining bird-watching with cycling, the best time to visit the park is between mid-October and mid-March. With your binoculars you will see whistling swans, Canada and snow geese, and over 20 species of ducks. Though the birds are wild, you will find them nonchalant about your presence. Their animal sixth sense tells them that they will not be harmed at the refuge. There are even traffic signs that warn of goose crossings. My friend George Demko and I cycled through the refuge in late September, and we passed within 10 feet of large flocks of geese. Out in the fields and farms, however, these honkers won't even let you come within a hundred yards before they take flight!

Blackwater is a large refuge and retains its primordial wildness. Try to imagine 15,615 acres composed of rich tidal marshes, freshwater ponds, and mixed woodlands. Blackwater is also a haven for endangered species, like the peregrine falcon and the Delmarva fox squirrel. Blackwater's importance to me, however, is that it is one of the few places on the Atlantic coast where you can see an American bald eagle in the wild.

To get to Blackwater Refuge by car, take MD 16 out of Cambridge from US 50. Head south 5 miles on MD 16 to Church Creek. From Church Creek follow MD 335 for 8 miles, to Key Wallace Road. Turn left on Key Wallace Road and follow the signs to the refuge.

Short-loop Tour—Directions for the Ride

0.0 *Blackwater Wildfowl Refuge visitors center. Park your car here. Bike out to Key Wallace Road, turn right, and continue to Wild-life Drive.*

1.7 *Turn right on Wildlife Drive.*

This is the beginning of the short bike loop through the park. On your right will be the park executive building. Watch out for traffic jams caused by the geese!

2.0 *Turn left to go to the observation tower.*

This 50-foot tower is a must-see on your tour. Climb it to the top and you will have one of the most impressive panoramic views on the Chesapeake shore. The marsh and water stretch off into the vast distance. Heron dive sharply into the water for fish, and hawks circle warily. Your best time at the tower is early morning or sunset when all the birds are roosting in the marsh.

From the tower, retrace your route 0.25 mile and turn left on the marsh trail.

Canada geese at the Blackwater Wildfowl Refuge
(*courtesy of the Maryland Department of Tourism*)

Although it is a designated bike trail, you will share it with automobiles. The trail takes you across the marsh and past fields planted in sorghum, a favorite waterfowl food. It was on this trail that we spotted a bald eagle.

5.2 *Turn right at the stop sign onto Key Wallace Road and return to the visitors center.*

5.5 *Return to the visitors parking lot.*

While you will have hardly broken a sweat on this loop, you will have seen one of the most impressive waterfowl refuges in America.

Long-loop Tour

Now that the easy loop through the refuge has whetted your appetite for a bigger ride through this 15,000-acre wonderland of water and salt marsh, you are ready for a more adventurous route.

Before starting out, check your tools and provisions. Make sure that you have extra tubes, a good bike pump, tools, and water. You will be traveling through the wilds of the south Dorchester County marshlands, one of the most remote areas of Chesapeake Bay country. There are very few gas stations, pay phones, or houses along this route. For most of this loop, it will be just you, your bike, and the marsh. Don't throw caution to the wind just because the refuge seems so beautiful and the highway so inviting. If you have to walk out of Blackwater Refuge with your bike, it can be a very long walk indeed.

Directions for the Ride

0.0 Blackwater Wildfowl Refuge visitors center. From the center parking lot, turn right onto Key Wallace Drive.

1.0 Turn right on Maple Dam Road.

Here you will make a long and solitary crossing of the middle of the refuge and Blackwater Marsh.

3.4 Turn right on Andrews Road.

12.3 Turn right on Crapo Road/MD 336.

21.8 At the hamlet of Crossroads, turn right on Church Creek Road/MD 335.

23.0 Turn right on Key Wallace Drive.

24.0 Blackwater Wildfowl Refuge visitors center.

Bicycle Repair Services

None on this route.

Attractions

Wild Goose Brewery (410-221-1121), 20 Washington St., Cambridge, MD. After a good bike ride across the marsh, you may wish to return to Cambridge and visit the Wild Goose. This popular microbrewery makes excellent English ale and porter and is open for tours daily until 3 PM.

Lodging

Loblolly Landings and Lodge (410-397-3033), 2142 Liners Rd., Church Creek, MD 21622. 2 rooms, private baths.

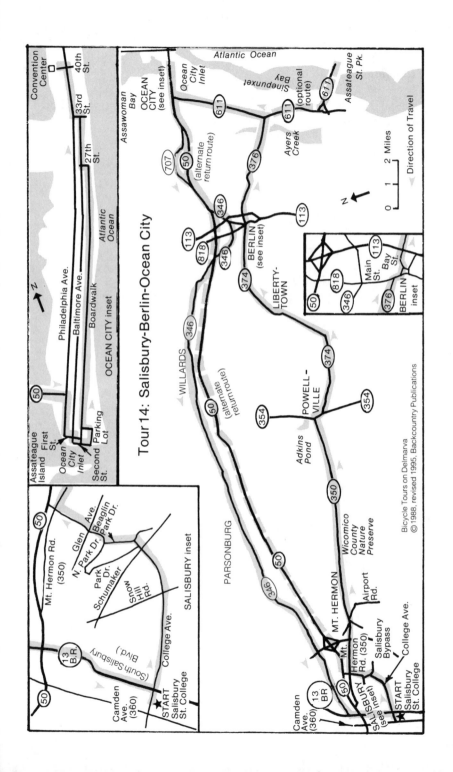

Tour 14: Salisbury-Berlin-Ocean City

Bicycle Tours on Delmarva
©1988, revised 1995, Backcountry Publications

14
Salisbury–Berlin–Ocean City

Distance: *35.4 miles one way*
Terrain: *Flat countryside*
Location: *Wicomico and Worcester Counties, Maryland*
Special features: *Salisbury, Berlin, Ocean City*

The trip to Ocean City from Salisbury is an excellent morning's sprint that can easily be accomplished in any season of the year. You will pass through countryside and along highways that, during midweek at least, are deserted country lanes. Even on a weekend in summer, this route is uncrowded and remains the quintessential cyclist's route to the sea. Country hamlets like Powellville still retain their vitality, and country stores are important social centers. Berlin, long chafing under its reputation as a stagnant farm town, is at last stirring. Berlin's business community today is lively and buoyant; hopes in the region are high that the westward expansion of Ocean City's resort prosperity will have a positive impact on local life. Also, Berlin is proud to be the birthplace of Stephen Decatur, one of early America's most daring naval war heroes.

Compared to Berlin, Ocean City is a neon giant dominating the economy of Worcester County. In winter, Ocean City is a sleepy seaside town of a few thousand. Come summer, however, Ocean City becomes a teeming resort metropolis hosting more than 225,000 people during any given week. While some visitors may deplore Ocean City's Coney Island atmosphere, others find it the ideal vacation playground. If anything, the resort demonstrates the old axiom that there is no accounting for popular tastes. There are many facets to Ocean City's character. In summer it is a kind of Peter Pan resort, dedicated to the needs and entertainment of the youth of Maryland and beyond. Later, as the tourist season slows around Labor Day, the resort appeals more to families looking for a seaside holiday on a budget. As October looms, the ocean breezes are still warm, and large numbers of retirees flock to the resort for what the Ocean City community refers to as "the second season."

Whether it is June or November, Ocean City's mild climate, surf, and boardwalk attract visitors. While Ocean City may not be the resort of your dreams, there is nonetheless something here to appeal to every taste and outlook.

Directions for the Ride

0.0 *This ride begins at the intersection of College and Camden Avenues in Salisbury at the campus of Salisbury State College. In summer, parking is easily available on side streets near the college, and motels and restaurants are nearby on US 13 South. Take College Avenue east from the intersection of Camden and College Avenues. Cross US Business Route 13 while continuing on College Avenue, which eventually becomes Beaglin Park Drive.*

3.4 *Continue to the end of Beaglin Park Drive and turn right onto Mt. Hermon Road/MD 350.*

5.4 *Pass through the hamlet of Mt. Hermon. At the intersection of Airport Road, where you will spot Ward's Cash Market, continue on MD 350 east through the Wicomico County Nature Preserve.*

The highway becomes a shady lane, with bird life replacing motor traffic. On both sides of the highway, the land becomes spongy, a reflection of the extending swamp and marsh that are so pervasive on the Eastern Shore.

13.8 *Enter Powellville.*

During World War II, Powellville had a large camp of conscientious objectors, some of whom worked on highway construction and swamp drainage projects. Boasting two general stores, Powellville is an excellent place to stop for a cold drink or morning coffee. Human-made Adkins Pond, with its tiny park, is within easy strolling distance of the general stores.

The harbor of Ocean City, Maryland (*photo by Orlando V. Wootten*)

14.4 *At the intersection of MD 350 and MD 354, turn right on MD 354.*

14.8 *Turn left on MD 374. If you miss this turn for Ocean City, you will end up in Snow Hill.*

19.5 *Pass through the hamlet of Libertytown.*

24.1 *Enter Berlin.*

The town's original name was Burleigh, which time and local speech corrupted to Berlin. In the 19th century, Berlin was a famous blacksmithing center for the Eastern Shore farm community. The shady winding streets still have many antebellum homes. Of late, this little town has undergone some gentrification. The people here are friendly and the local restaurants are inexpensive and serve good regional fare.

24.9 *At Farlow's Pharmacy on Main Street make a sharp right turn.*

Then quickly bear left at the Peninsula Bank. You will now be on Bay Street/MD 376. Take care not to miss this turn!

25.3 *There is a traffic light at the intersection of MD 376 and US 113. Cross US 113 and continue on MD 376.*

28.8 *Ayers Creek.*

Stop at the bridge and gaze at this large tidal creek with fine homes perched proudly on its banks. The creek is a favorite with ospreys and sea hawks.

29.5 *At the junction of MD 376 and MD 611 you have two options.*

You can turn right and follow MD 611 to Assateague State Park and its beaches (4.6 miles). There is a public campground at Assateague State Park, though it is often quite crowded in the summer. Also, mind the sand flies!

Your other option (the remainder of this tour) is to turn left on MD 611 and continue on to Ocean City. Caution: MD 611 is busy in the summer, especially where it passes Ocean City Airport.

33.5 *At the intersection of MD 611 and US 50, turn right onto US 50. Cross the drawbridge into Ocean City. Because of the heavy traffic on this bridge, use the sidewalk. The bridge sidewalk is fenced off to protect bikers, walkers, and anglers from auto traffic.*

35.4 *After the bridge, turn right onto Philadelphia Avenue. Proceed on Philadelphia Avenue to First Street. You are now at the Ocean City Inlet.*

The Ocean City Lifesaving Station Museum will be on your immediate left. The inlet has a fascinating parade of boats going from Assowoman Bay to the Atlantic Ocean, and the Lifesaving Museum has a well-organized collection of memorabilia on ocean rescue work in the late 19th and early 20th centuries.

Turn left on First Street and follow it into Ocean City's huge parking lot. The Ocean City boardwalk begins at the north end of the lot.

Your experience in Ocean City will be what you make of it. Some see the resort as the confirmation of their worst fears about resort tackiness in America. Others are enthralled by the town's boardwalk promenade and active social life. At this resort you'll see a cavalcade of humanity—from taffy-chewing dowagers to punk motorcyclists with green hair and pierced noses. Good luck!

SIDE TRIP: Boardwalk Minitour. While you are in Ocean City, you will want to bike on the boardwalk to enjoy the beach scenery and savor the Atlantic breeze. Please note that you cannot bike on the boardwalk after 10 am during the Memorial Day–Labor Day season. The postseason period has less pedestrian traffic, and you can ride on the boardwalk at any time.

From the inlet parking lot, begin your minitour at the Lifesaving Station Museum. Proceed up the parking lot toward the giant Ferris wheel. Turn left at Pier Entertainment and right onto the boardwalk. Follow the boardwalk 2.3 miles to its end. From the boardwalk's end go left on 33rd Street. At the intersection of Baltimore Avenue and 33rd Street, turn right on Baltimore Avenue. Ride to 40th Street and turn into the mammoth Ocean City Convention Center. The resort's Visitors and Information Bureau is located there, and you can obtain literature about all of the resort activities. Retrace your steps back to 33rd Street and the boardwalk and return to the inlet parking lot.

A Note for the Return Ride

If you are in a hurry to return to Salisbury, the quickest route back is US 50 West. This dual highway, however, carries heavy traffic in summer. A more enjoyable route is MD 707, which you can pick up 1.9 miles out of Ocean City off US 50 on your right. Just before Berlin, MD 707 ends; turn left onto US 50 and look for its intersection with MD 346. Follow MD 346 out of Berlin to Willards, Parsonburg, and finally Salisbury. In downtown Salisbury, turn left onto South Salisbury Boulevard/ US Business Route 13 and continue on to College Avenue. Turn right to Salisbury State College and the end of your ride.

Bicycle Repair Services

Bike World (410-289-2587), 10 Caroline St., Ocean City, MD.

Continental Cycles (410-524-1313), 7203 Coastal Hwy., Ocean City, MD.

Attractions

Berlin Historic District. Turn-of-the-century houses and commercial district: antiques shops, the restored Victorian Atlantic Hotel, Federal-era homes.

Lodging

Atlantic Hotel Inn and Restaurant (410-641-3589), 2 N. Main St., Berlin, MD 21811. 126 rooms, private baths.

Atlantic House (410-289-2333), 501 N. Baltimore Ave., Ocean City, MD 21842. 14 rooms, private baths.

Econo Lodge (410-524-5634), 102 60th St., Ocean City, MD 21842.

Holland House (410-641-1956), 5 Bay St., Berlin, MD 21811. 5 rooms.

The Taylor House B&B (410-289-1177), 1101 Baltimore Ave., Ocean City, MD 21842. 4 rooms, private baths. Good food and inexpensive rates make Taylor House one of the best touring values in Ocean City.

15
Salisbury Loop

Distance: 13.7 miles
Terrain: Flat countryside
Location: Wicomico County, Maryland
Special features: Salisbury, Pemberton Hall Plantation, Upper Ferry

This loop is designed to acquaint you with the countryside surrounding the city of Salisbury. Using the city's motels and restaurants as a base, you can spend a delightful weekend cycling virtually in any direction, from Berlin and Ocean City to the east to Princess Anne in the south.

On this trip you will be cycling primarily through the west side of Wicomico County. Much of your riding will parallel the Wicomico River, and you will have an opportunity to pause along this route and watch the river traffic. Should you desire to cruise on the river, the steamer *Maryland Lady* plies the Wicomico on luncheon and tourist excursions twice a day during the May-September season. Despite Salisbury's urban growth, it is still surprisingly easy to get out into the countryside. On a sunny Saturday afternoon it is great fun to pack a picnic lunch and cycle out of town to the Pemberton Hall Historical Park.

This loop is very popular with racing cyclists who use it as a training run. Expect to be passed every now and then by a group of blazing cyclists! Also, traffic is light on the highways you will be following.

This tour begins at the parking garage on North Division Street in downtown Salisbury. The garage is located across the street from the library and the town fire station. Easy access to parking makes this an excellent departure point for your tour. To get there, turn off US 50 at the traffic light onto North Division Street. If you are coming from Annapolis and the west, turn right; if you are coming from the east, turn left.

North-south travelers can enter Salisbury on Main Street at the traffic

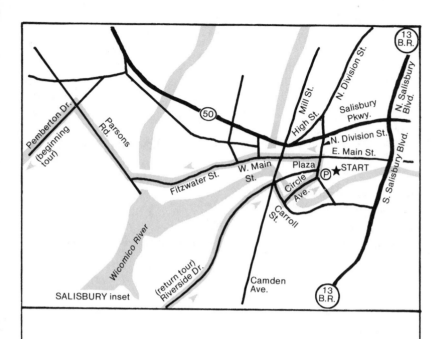

SALISBURY inset

Pemberton Dr. (beginning tour)

Parsons Rd.

Wicomico River

Fitzwater St.

W. Main St.

Carroll St.

Camden Ave.

(return tour) Riverside Dr.

Circle Ave.

Plaza

E. Main St.

N. Division St.

Salisbury Pkwy.

High St.

Mill St.

N. Division St.

N. Salisbury Blvd.

S. Salisbury Blvd.

13 B.R.

13 B.R.

★ START

P

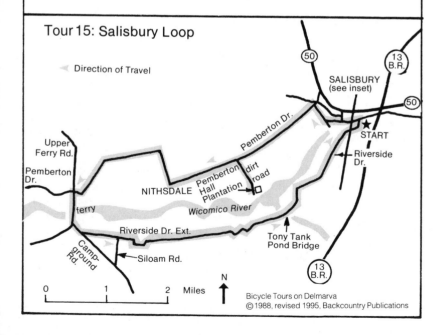

Tour 15: Salisbury Loop

◄ Direction of Travel

50

13 B.R.

SALISBURY (see inset)

50

★ START

Pemberton Dr.

Riverside Dr.

Upper Ferry Rd.

Pemberton Dr.

ferry

NITHSDALE

Pemberton Hall Plantation

dirt road

Wicomico River

Riverside Dr. Ext.

Tony Tank Pond Bridge

Camp-ground Rd.

Siloam Rd.

13 B.R.

0   1   2   Miles

N

Bicycle Tours on Delmarva
© 1988, revised 1995, Backcountry Publications

light intersection of US 13 and Main Street. If you are coming from the north, turn right on Main Street; from the south, turn left. Proceed 0.5 mile up Main Street to the T and traffic light at Salisbury's downtown plaza. Turn left on North Division Street. The parking garage will be 1 block on your left.

Directions for the Ride

0.0   *Once you have parked your car, turn right and proceed back up North Division Street to the traffic light and Salisbury Plaza.*

Once a traffic thoroughfare, the plaza is now an open pedestrian mall with park benches, bubbling water fountains, and tastefully decorated stores. Sorry, biking on the plaza is prohibited, and you will have to walk your bike a short distance.

0.2   *At the end of the plaza mount your bike and head straight toward the traffic light. Cross Mill Street and continue straight ahead on West Main Street. You will cross a small drawbridge.*

0.4   *The entrance to the Port of Salisbury Marina on the Wicomico River will be on your left.*

This new city-developed marina is the home port of the *Maryland Lady* and a large flotilla of sailing and power vessels.

0.7   *Chesapeake Shipbuilding Inc. will be on your left.*

Salisbury's shipyards played an important role in the economy of the 19th-century Eastern Shore. Lately, the founding of this new shipyard has reestablished Salisbury as a center for the construction of Chesapeake vessels. Most of the ships built here are "love boats," cruising vessels for the bay and elsewhere.

1.2   *At the stop sign, turn left onto Pemberton Drive. The Shore Stop convenience market will be on your left.*

3.2   *Pemberton Hall Plantation and Historical Park. To get to the plantation, turn left into the park entrance and proceed down a dirt lane for 0.75 mile.*

Here you will see a substantial gambrel-roofed brick house built in 1741. The date is on the gable. In the 18th century this was the plantation of Isaac Handy and his family. The socially prominent Handys played an important role on the Eastern Shore during the colonial and Revolutionary periods. The architecture of Pemberton Hall has a Flemish quality that makes it distinctive in the region. Rescued from near ruin by the dedicated Pemberton Hall Historical Society, the plantation is now a major tourist attraction in Wicomico County. Each October, Pemberton Hall hosts a colonial fair that includes music and dancing from the 18th century, colonial craft displays, colonial cooking, and horsemanship skills reflective of the Revolutionary era. The plantation has paths, picnic areas, and vistas of the Wicomico River.

Go back to Pemberton Drive and turn left.

4.2   Nithsdale will be on your left.

Formerly a chicken farm, Nithsdale is now a housing development for the newly affluent of Salisbury. It was named by a Scottish planter after his native Nithsdale.

5.4   Hollywood Farm will be on your left. Continue on Pemberton Drive.

6.7   At the intersection of Pemberton Drive and Upper Ferry Road, turn left onto Upper Ferry Road.

7.0   Upper Ferry is one of two small cable ferries still working in Wicomico County, and it will give you a short, though delightful, crossing of the river.

A ferry has operated here since the colonial period. It derives its name from the fact that it is upriver from the other cable ferry at Whitehaven on the Wicomico–Somerset County boundary. The ferry has its own idiosyncratic schedule. Between October 1 and February 29, the ferry runs 7 AM–5 PM. From March 1 to September 30, the ferry runs 7 AM–6 PM. The ferry closes at 1 PM on Saturday and is closed on Sunday, so plan accordingly. The best part is that the ferry is free.

7.2   After the ferry crossing, the highway forks. Take the left fork onto Campground Road.

7.4   Turn left on Riverside Drive Extension.

8.1   At the stop sign and intersection of Riverside Drive and

A colonial fair at Pemberton Hall Plantation

Siloam Road, keep left onto Riverside Drive.

10.0 Silver Run Community will be on your left.

11.3 Cross Tony Tank Pond Bridge, where there is a scenic vista of the Wicomico River.

13.2 St. Francis Catholic Church will be on your right.

13.6 At the intersection and traffic light, turn right on Carroll Street. Then take a quick left at the bridge across a tributary of Wicomico River onto Circle Avenue. Continue up Circle Avenue toward the parking garage.

13.7 At the intersection and traffic light of Circle Avenue and North Division Street, cross North Division Street and enter the parking garage. This is the end of your journey.

Bicycle Repair Services

Salisbury Schwinn Cyclery (410-546-4747), 1404 S. Salisbury Blvd., Salisbury, MD.

The Bikesmith (410-749-2453), 1053 N. Salisbury Blvd., Salisbury, MD.

Attractions

Ward Museum of Wildfowl Art (410-742-4988), 909 S. Shumaker Dr., Salisbury, MD. Contemporary bird carvings, antique decoys, the history and development of decoy carving in America, and displays of current champion decoys. Open Monday through Saturday 9–5.

Lodging

Temple Hill Motel (410-742-3284), 1510 S. Salisbury Blvd. (0.5 mile south of Salisbury State College), Salisbury, MD 21801.

Days Inn (410-749-6200), US 13, N. Salisbury Blvd., Salisbury, MD.

16
Salisbury–Princess Anne Loop

Distance: *27 miles*
Terrain: *Flat*
Location: *Wicomico and Somerset Counties, Maryland*
Special features: *Salisbury City Park and Zoo, Salisbury State College, Allen, Princess Anne*

Salisbury, the largest town on Maryland's Eastern Shore, is an excellent base for those cyclists who wish to explore the central Chesapeake Bay area. Although Salisbury is rapidly growing as a commercial and medical center, the city retains its small-town ambience. Lawyers and businesspeople take long lunches at downtown restaurants, and the pace of life is decidedly unhurried. Salisbury is the seat of Wicomico County, and its location on the Wicomico River has made it an important commercial entrepôt since the 18th century.

The Newtown area of the city has many fine Victorian mansions and homes that have been tastefully restored. Also, the Salisbury City Park and Zoo offers broad lawns, shady paths, and cool river vistas for tired cyclists. In summer the *Maryland Lady,* a replica of a 19th-century Eastern Shore steamboat, regularly plies the waters of the Wicomico River on dining and sightseeing cruises.

Salisbury is also the home of Salisbury State College, a liberal arts school that serves as the town's cultural center. The college houses the Ward Foundation Museum, which is dedicated to keeping alive the Chesapeake Bay folk art of handcrafted duck and goose decoys.

Heading south on your tour, you will pass through the sleepy village of Allen and then directly on to Princess Anne. Still possessing an abundance of colonial charm, Princess Anne is a delight for the American history buff or those who have a fine eye for architecture. Manokin Pres-

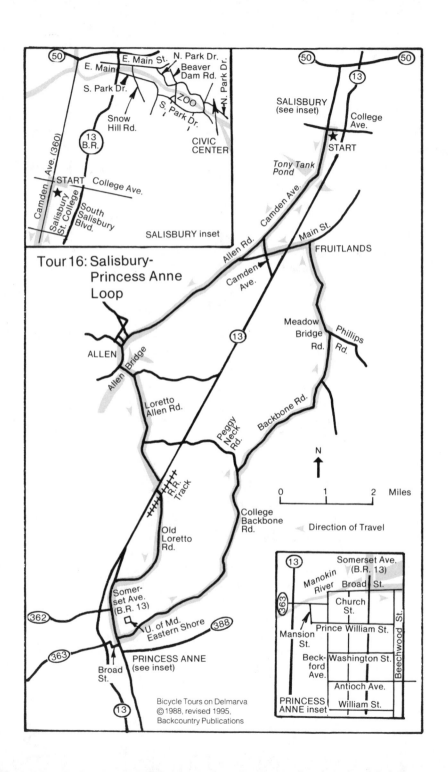

Tour 16: Salisbury-Princess Anne Loop

Salisbury inset:
50
E. Main St.
E. Main
N. Park Dr.
Beaver Dam Rd.
S. Park Dr.
ZOO
S. Park Dr.
N. Park Dr.
13 B.R.
Snow Hill Rd.
CIVIC CENTER
Camden Ave. (360)
START
Salisbury St. College
College Ave.
South Salisbury Blvd.
SALISBURY inset

50
13
50
SALISBURY (see inset)
College Ave.
START
Tony Tank Pond
Camden Ave.
Allen Rd.
Main St.
FRUITLANDS
Camden Ave.
Meadow Bridge Rd.
Phillips Rd.
13
ALLEN
Allen Bridge
Loretto Allen Rd.
Peggy Neck Rd.
Backbone Rd.
N
0   1   2   Miles
R.R. Track
Old Loretto Rd.
College Backbone Rd.
◄ Direction of Travel
362
Somerset Ave. (B.R. 13)
U. of Md. Eastern Shore
388
363
Broad St.
PRINCESS ANNE (see inset)
13

Bicycle Tours on Delmarva
© 1988, revised 1995,
Backcountry Publications

Princess Anne inset:
13
Somerset Ave. (B.R. 13)
Manokin River
Broad St.
363
Church St.
Mansion St.
Prince William St.
Beechwood St.
Beckford Ave.
Washington St.
Antioch Ave.
William St.
PRINCESS ANNE inset

byterian Church on Somerset Avenue dates from 1765, and Somerset County has been the cradle of American Presbyterianism since Reverend Francis Makemie preached here in the late 17th century. Tunstall Cottage at Broad and Church Streets dates from 1705 and is the oldest inhabited dwelling in Princess Anne. The town is also the seat of Somerset County, founded in 1666 and one of the oldest political units in Maryland.

Prince William Street contains some of the finest antebellum architecture to be seen anywhere in the country. At the head of Prince William Street stands the sprawling Teackle Mansion with its elegant gardens. Built in 1801 by Littleton Dennis Teackle, a wealthy merchant-planter and associate of Thomas Jefferson, the mansion is a copy of a Scottish manor house.

After touring Princess Anne, stop at the Washington Hotel. This inn has been host to weary travelers since 1744. Afterwards, cycle through the beautiful Georgian-style campus of the University of Maryland, Eastern Shore. I have included an alternate return route map for those wishing to cycle back to Salisbury.

In my opinion, the best time to take this loop is early in the autumn when the weather is cooler and the heat and humidity of summer are but a memory. (*One caution:* you will encounter country dogs on this route, but they are easily handled by experienced cyclists. See the Helpful Hints section in the book's introduction.)

Directions for the Ride

0.0 *This tour begins at the entrance of Salisbury State College on Camden Avenue. Ample parking is available on side streets, and motel accommodations are close by. From Salisbury State College head south on Camden Avenue.*

1.0 *On both your right and left observe the large ponds created by the New Deal WPA in the 1930s. You are now at Tony Tank.* This site bears the corruption of an old Algonquian name now lost to history. Notice the restored colonnaded late-19th-century mansion on your right. Tony Tank is currently an affluent enclave for the elite of Salisbury. You may wish to turn right on Tony Tank Lane and sample the wooded atmosphere of this quiet neighborhood.

2.5   *Turn right off Camden Avenue onto Allen Road Cutoff. The Farm House Tavern will be on your right.*

6.1   *Enter the village of Allen, a quaint hamlet located on the boundary of Wicomico and Somerset Counties.*

Allen traces its settlement to 1667. Many of the clapboard houses have been restored, including Virginia Cottage, a well-known Colonial manor house that will be on your left as you cycle through Allen. While at Allen, stop at the Allen Post Office and Country Store, a remnant of the kind of country store that prevailed in the Chesapeake country in the 1930s. It is a good place to replenish supplies and liquids, and many cyclists stop here en route to Princess Anne.

6.8   *Allen Bridge. Here you have a good view of a large dammed pond that is a delight for weekend anglers. It is a good place to stop for a picnic lunch. Shortly after the bridge, the road forks. Continue right on Loretto Allen Road.*

9.6   *At the intersection of Allen Road and US 13, cross US 13 and proceed across railroad tracks onto Old Loretto Road, which will take you to the outskirts of Princess Anne.*

12.2   *Turn left at the stop sign onto Somerset Avenue/US Business Route 13.*

13.3   *Manokin Presbyterian Church will be on your right.*

13.5   *The intersection and traffic light of Somerset Avenue and Broad Street mark the downtown area of the village of Princess Anne. Spend some time touring Princess Anne.*

A Note for the Return Ride

13.5   *At the intersection and traffic light on Somerset Avenue and Broad Street in Princess Anne, turn left and head east on University Drive toward the University of Maryland, Eastern Shore.*

Founded in 1886 as Princess Anne Academy, an industrial and agricultural training institute for blacks, the University of Mary-

Campus of the University of Maryland, Eastern Shore, in Princess Anne, Maryland (*photo by Orlando V. Wootten*)

land, Eastern Shore, is now an undergraduate and research component of the University of Maryland system. The campus is nationally known for its research on crops, poultry, nutrition, and Chesapeake Bay marine science.

If you do not wish to enter the campus, turn left at the stop sign onto the university loop. If you cross the campus, enter the quadrangle. At the library rejoin the service road to the campus farm.

14.3 At the stop sign, the loop ends at the University of Maryland Agricultural Teaching Center and campus farm. Turn left at the stop sign onto College Backbone Road.

18.5 The junction of Peggy Neck Road, College Backbone Road, and Backbone Road is confusing. Examine the signs carefully and make sure that you turn right onto Backbone Road.

21.3 At the stop sign, turn left off of Backbone Road onto Meadowbridge Road.

22.3 At the intersection of Phillips Road and Meadowbridge Road, keep left on Meadowbridge Road.

24.0 Meadowbridge Road merges with East Main Street in the town of Fruitland.

24.6 At the intersection of Main Street and US 13, cross US 13 and continue on West Main Street.

25.0 At the intersection and flashing light at West Main Street and Camden Avenue, turn right on Camden Avenue.

27.0 Approach the entrance of Salisbury State College and the end of your tour.

Bicycle Repair Services

Salisbury Schwinn (410-546-4747), 1404 S. Salisbury Blvd., Salisbury, MD.

Lodging

Allendale Cottage B&B (410-860-2800), 331 Allen Rd., Allen, MD 21810. 2 rooms.

Hayman House B&B (410-651-2753), 117 Prince William St., Princess Anne, MD 21853. 4 rooms, private baths. This elegantly appointed Victorian townhouse (circa 1898) offers great comfort and value. If you love Victorian antiques and furnishings, you will love this place.

Hospitality House (410-651-6565), University of Maryland, Eastern Shore, Princess Anne, MD 21853. A tourist bargain, this hotel is run by the university's School of Hotel and Restaurant Management. It can only be booked for large groups.

Washington Hotel (410-651-2525), 32 Somerset Ave., Princess Anne, MD 21853.

17
Princess Anne–Deal Island

Distance: *37.5 miles round trip*
Terrain: *Rolling hills and marsh*
Location: *Somerset County, Maryland*
Special features: *Deal Island Wildlife Management Area, Reverend Joshua Thomas Chapel, Wenona*

Heading due west on MD 363 out of Princess Anne, you will have the splendid opportunity of cycling across one of the great marshes of Chesapeake Bay country. The low and swampy terrain easily gives way to the marsh that stretches to the horizon. Turkey buzzards circle lazily in the sky, and on a crisp fall day the silence of this vast natural area can be awe-inspiring.

One note of caution: The trip across the marsh is strenuous in summer, although it is little more than 14 miles to the Deal Island Bridge. The greenhead fly, a summer denizen of the Deal Island Marsh, can be a painful nuisance. My son Stewart and I foolishly rode across the marsh at the beginning of August when we thought that the greenheads would not be too bad. The flies swarmed all over us, however, and my T-shirt was literally black with them. We were bitten so badly that we were close to tears. The one bright spot of the marsh crossing was that we averaged nearly 18 miles an hour; we were eager to leave those greenheads behind!

Almost miraculously, the greenheads disappear around the end of September, and from October through April you can enjoy the spectacular beauty of the marsh and be free of insects.

There's history aplenty on this trip as the Deal Island area was one of the first to be settled in this part of the Chesapeake in the late 17th century. Deal Island (once known as Devil's Island) was the home of the great evangelical Methodist preacher, Joshua Thomas. This parson of

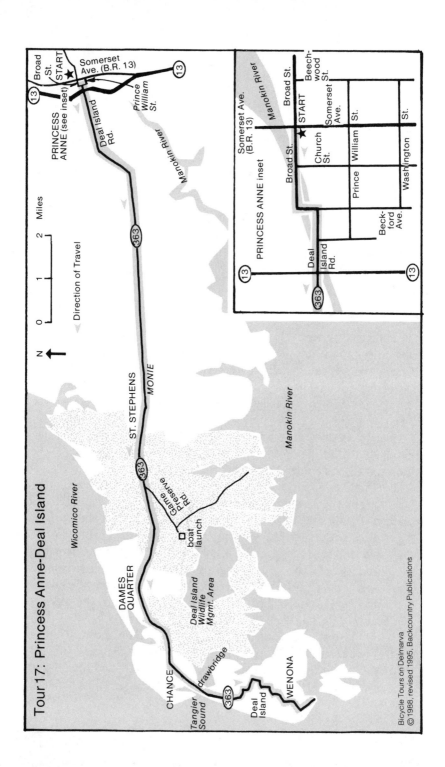

Tour 17: Princess Anne-Deal Island

Bicycle Tours on Delmarva
© 1988, revised 1995, Backcountry Publications

the islands took the half-savage fisher folk of Tangier Island and Deal Island and converted them to Methodism. Deal Islanders were descendants of convicts and indentured servants who had been transported to Maryland Plantation, and they rejected the colder tenets of the Anglican faith. But when Joshua Thomas preached of fire and damnation, using the metaphor and experience of life on the sea, the islanders flocked to the fold.

During the American Revolution, Deal Island was a pirate haven for picaroons who preyed on the naval commerce of the Revolutionary government and hoped for a Tory victory. Deal Island sits astride Tangier Sound in the Chesapeake and has always been a community of watermen. Although life dependent on the Chesapeake Bay can be tough, Deal Islanders have an earthy sense of humor. A general store in Wenona boasts that the establishment "is not quite at the end of the world, but you can see it from here."

Deal Island is also the home port of the rapidly disappearing fleet of skipjacks. These one-masted sailboats are licensed to pull a dredge across the Chesapeake Bay bottom for oysters. The work is hard and dangerous and fewer skipjacks go out during oyster season each year. Now there are fewer than 30 boats actually working the oyster trade.

Either in port or at sea, the skipjacks are beautiful and serve as a reminder of the 19th-century nautical tradition in fishing that has practically vanished along the Atlantic seaboard. When you go to Wenona, take time to look at and photograph these proud but declining vessels. They may not be around when you next return.

Directions for the Ride

0.0 *Our trip begins at the traffic light intersection of Broad Street and Somerset Avenue in Princess Anne. You can easily park your car on any street in the village. Follow Broad Street west past Tunstall Cottage, the oldest Colonial residence in Princess Anne.*

0.2 *Turn right on Deal Island Road, which becomes MD 363.*

0.3 *At the intersection of US 13 and MD 363, cross US 13 and head straight on MD 363 for Deal Island. MD 363 passes*

Teackle Mansion in Princess Anne, Maryland (*photo by Orlando V. Wootten*)

through farmland and low forest that gradually recede into
the marsh.

8.0 The great Deal Island marsh stretches far to the horizon. The
marsh teems with wildlife and is the beginning of the food
cycle of the Chesapeake Bay.

10.3 SIDE TRIP: Just ahead lies the Deal Island Wildlife Management Area. Its 10,200-plus acres of marsh abound in wildlife.

Turn left onto Game Preserve Road. This dirt road ends at a
small boat-launching site, but you have an uninterrupted view
of the marsh far away from the sound of motor traffic. When
you return to the highway, turn left on Deal Island Road.

11.3 Enter Dames Quarter, once called Damned Quarter, a farming
and fishing village that has a small marina and restaurant.

After passing through the hamlets of Monie and St. Stephens, you
will think Dames Quarter is a metropolis!

14.0 Come to the village of Chance and the entry to the drawbridge that will take you to Deal Island.

15.1 At the end of the drawbridge enter Deal Island.

The Reverend Joshua Thomas Chapel and its graveyard dominate
Deal Island, and it is easy to tell by the surrounding churches that
this is a solid Methodist community. Joshua Thomas preached to

the British soldiers on Tangier Island during the War of 1812 and told them that he had been told by God that the British would not rule the Chesapeake Bay. Thomas died in 1853 and is buried in a vault beside the chapel. His epitaph reads: "Come all my friends as you pass by. Behold the place where I do lie. Once as you so was I. Remember you are born to die."

As you cycle across the island, you will notice that the road takes many twists and turns that seem strange until you realize how low the ground is. The road on the island was built on the highest ground to prevent flooding at high tides.

18.7 Wenona Harbor and boat ramp.

This fishing community provides harbor for the last of the rapidly dwindling skipjack oyster-dredging sailboats. There is a general store here, and you can purchase provisions and eat lunch. Lock up your bike, walk along the wharf, and gaze at the skipjacks or walk out to the shoreline of the island and search for arrowheads and potsherds.

A Note for the Return Ride

As they say down here on Deal Island, "Honey, you'll have to go back the same way you come in, 'less you want to swim to Crisfield with that bike."

Bicycle Repair Services

None on this route.

Attractions

Princess Anne Historical District (1-800-521-9189), Princess Anne, MD. Includes Teackle Mansion (1801), Manokin Presbyterian Church (1765), Tunstall Cottage (1733), Washington Hotel (1744), and Boxwood Gardens (1842). Free self-guided tour brochure available.

The Reverend Joshua Thomas Chapel and graveyard on Deal Island, Maryland

Lodging

Hayman House Bed and Breakfast (410-651-2753), 30491 Prince William St., Princess Anne, MD 21853. 4 rooms, private baths. This B&B is tastefully decorated in the Victorian style and is a favorite with cyclists. Advance booking suggested.

Washington Hotel (410-651-2525), 32 Somerset Ave., Princess Anne, MD 21853.

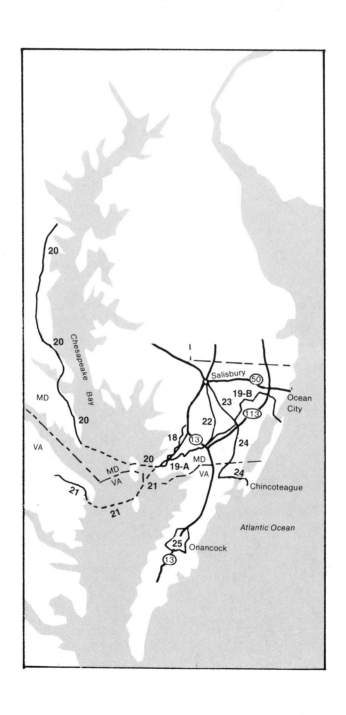

THE LOWER CHESAPEAKE

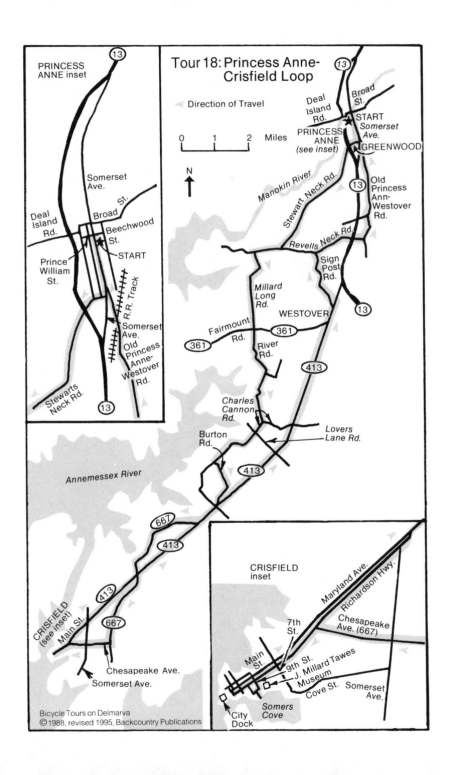

PRINCESS ANNE inset

Tour 18: Princess Anne-Crisfield Loop

Direction of Travel

0   1   2   Miles

N

Somerset Ave.

Deal Island Rd.

Broad St.

Beechwood St.

START

Prince William St.

R.R. Track

Somerset Ave.

Old Princess Anne-Westover Rd.

Stewarts Neck Rd.

13

Deal Island Rd.

Broad St.

START

Somerset Ave.

PRINCESS ANNE (see inset)

GREENWOOD

Manokin River

Stewart Neck Rd.

Old Princess Ann-Westover Rd.

Revells Neck Rd.

Sign Post Rd.

Millard Long Rd.

WESTOVER

Fairmount Rd.

361

361

River Rd.

413

Charles Cannon Rd.

Burton Rd.

Lovers Lane Rd.

413

Annemessex River

667

413

413

667

CRISFIELD (see inset)

Main St.

Chesapeake Ave.

Somerset Ave.

CRISFIELD inset

Maryland Ave.

Richardson Hwy.

Chesapeake Ave. (667)

7th St.

9th St.

J. Millard Tawes Museum

Cove St.

Somerset Ave.

Main St.

City Dock

Somers Cove

Bicycle Tours on Delmarva
©1988, revised 1995, Backcountry Publications

18

Princess Anne–Crisfield Loop

Distance: *45 miles*
Terrain: *Flat with occasional marsh and riverfront*
Location: *Somerset County, Maryland*
Special features: *Princess Anne, Crisfield, Somers Cove Marina,*
J. Millard Tawes Museum

The Princess Anne–Crisfield loop is a cycle trip through time, taking bikers through the historic town of Princess Anne and across a region bisected by the Manokin and Annemessex Rivers. This area was settled in the 17th century by Quakers and political dissenters from the Eastern Shore of Virginia.

During the summer, this route can be exceedingly hot and humid, so pick a cool day for your ride or wait for autumn. Let two key regional festivals serve as your guide. On Labor Day weekend Crisfield hosts its annual National Hard Crab Derby and Fair, a major tourist attraction that features a contest where Chesapeake blue crabs race down an inclined platform to win prizes for their owners. There are also crab-picking contests, watercraft shows, and country and western music. As civic organizations sell steamed crabs and oyster sandwiches, the Derby is also an adventure in good eating. The 132-slip marina at Somers Cove is a favorite stopover for yachts that are cruising Chesapeake Bay.

In the second weekend of October, the village of Princess Anne welcomes over a thousand visitors for its annual Old Princess Anne Days. The town and surrounding area become one large open house, and visitors can see some of the oldest and most elegant plantations and manor houses in the Chesapeake region. Princess Anne celebrates its colonial heritage with militia musters, carriage rides, and a fox hunt.

The Princess Anne–Crisfield loop can be easily done in a day. Also, this loop is good preparation for other bike trips, such as Tours 17, 20, and 22. Take a weekend and reserve a room at the Washington Hotel in Princess Anne. This antique-filled inn has been in continuous operation since 1745. The inn has a double stairway to the second floor so that women who wore large hoop skirts could pass on the stairs without inconveniencing male guests.

Directions for the Ride

0.0   *Begin in Princess Anne at the Somerset County Court House at the corner of Somerset Avenue and Prince William Street. There is ample parking space on side streets. Head south on Somerset Avenue.*

0.7   *Turn right at the Highway Market next to the old warehouse of Kings Creek Cannery onto the beginning of Stewart Neck Road. Enter the Greenwood residential area.*

1.1   *You will come to US 13, the major north-south route on the Eastern Shore. Cross US 13 and continue on Stewart Neck Road.*

4.1   *Turn right at the stop sign on Revells Neck Road.*

5.7   *Turn left on Millard Long Road.*

8.2   *At the stop sign, Millard Long Road becomes River Road. Continue straight.*

You will travel through some of the beautiful marshlands of the Annemessex River.

11.3   *At the end of River Road, turn right on Charles Cannon Road.*

11.8   *The road forks here. Keep to the right and continue on Charles Cannon Road. (If you end up on Lovers Lane Road, you've missed the turn.)*

13.4   *You will reach an intersection and sign for Marshall's Seafood. Turn left on Burton Road.*

15.3   *Burton Road leads to MD 413, the Crisfield Highway. Turn right onto MD 413.*

16.0   *Turn right off MD 413 at the Texaco Convenience Store and*

Packing softshelled crabs at the John T. Handy Company
in Crisfield, Maryland (*photo by Orlando V. Wootten*)

follow MD 667/Ward-Crisfield Road to Crisfield.

19.0 At the intersection of MD 413 and MD 667, cross MD 413 and continue on MD 667.

22.0 Enter Crisfield. MD 667 becomes Chesapeake Avenue. At the stop sign, cross Somerset Avenue and continue on Chesapeake Avenue.

22.5 From Chesapeake Avenue, turn left on Maryland Avenue (also referred to as Main Street) and head toward the city municipal dock. At this point the highway has four lanes. During the summer, Crisfield is a busy town. Watch out for the seafood trucks!

23.3 Crisfield City Dock.

You are now in the most important area of town. This is the heart of the region's maritime commerce and the main street and side streets are lined with restaurants and seafood-packing houses. From the dock the view of Tangier Sound is excellent. On a clear day you can see Smith Island, 12 miles due west. The mail and passenger boats for Smith and Tangier Islands depart from here. (See this book's introduction for ferry schedules.)

A hundred years ago Crisfield prided itself on being the seafood capital of the world. During the heyday of the Chesapeake oyster industry, Crisfield watermen harvested millions of bushels of oysters out of Tangier Sound and shipped them fresh, frozen, or canned to American urban centers and beyond. In 1886, when Chesapeake watermen harvested a record 15 million bushels of oysters from the bay, Crisfield's canned oysters could be purchased in the silver towns of Nevada and in the posh groceries of London's Mayfair. With money to be made and the Chesapeake's mother lode to be looted, Crisfield grew to be a raucous boomtown reminiscent of those on the American frontier.

The oyster beds of Tangier Sound have long since been depleted, and the pace of Crisfield today is more settled. But the town still retains its hard-working salty openness. The oyster and crab packing houses still bustle with activity, especially in late morning when the watermen come to port with their catches.

To sample the maritime flavor of the town, stroll along the docks of Somers Cove Marina. (From the town dock, proceed up

Maryland Avenue/Main Street to Ninth Street and turn right.) Also, visit the J. Millard Tawes Museum with its historical displays of the culture of the Crisfield area.

Near the town dock is the popular Ice Cream Gallery. Located in a small alley behind a seafood warehouse, the gallery dispenses large amounts of ice cream to travel-weary cyclists, and the shop's dockside veranda is a favorite with boat watchers and dessert lovers alike.

A Note for the Return Ride

23.3 Head north from the town dock out of Crisfield on Richardson Highway, which parallels Maryland Avenue. The two roads eventually merge into MD 413.

37.2 Enter the hamlet of Westover. Turn left at a country church onto Sign Post Road.

39.1 Turn right at the stop sign onto Revells Neck Road. This road will take you past the sprawling Eastern Correctional Facility, one of the largest prisons in Maryland. (Nothing to worry about. Enjoy the scenery.)

40.3 Continue on Revells Neck Road to US 13. Cross US 13 and continue straight. A large grain elevator will be on your right.

40.8 At the end of Revells Neck Road, the highway comes to a T where there is a stop sign. Turn left. You will be on the Old Princess Anne–Westover Road, heading north to Princess Anne.

43.9 Cross the railroad tracks and at the stop sign turn right and continue into Princess Anne on Somerset Avenue.

45.0 Just past the courthouse on the left, the Washington Hotel marks the end of your journey.

Bicycle Repair Services

None on this route.

Attractions

For more information on the National Hard Crab Derby and Fair, or on Old Princess Anne Days, contact the Somerset County Bureau of Tourism (410-651-2968), PO Box 243, Princess Anne, MD 21853.

Governor J. Millard Tawes Museum (410-968-2501), Somers Cove Marina, Crisfield, MD 21817. Millard Tawes was governor of Maryland in the early 1960s and a friend of President Kennedy. The museum has exhibits pertaining to the late governor, local history, and the development of Crisfield's seafood industry.

Cruises leave daily from the Crisfield dock area for Smith Island and Tangier Island. See Tour 20 for details.

Ice Cream Alley, a delightful ice cream parlor near the Crisfield dock, is not to be missed by the weary cyclist. If you're starved for news, you can get *The Washington Post* or *The New York Times* from Karen Megronigle at In the News Bookstore, 940 West Main Street. Crisfield is a friendly place, and the natives will enjoy showing you their town.

Lodging

Hayman House Bed and Breakfast (410-651-2753), 30491 Prince William St., Princess Anne, MD 21853.

Islanders Bed and Breakfast (410-968-3314), 26391 Mariners Road, Crisfield, MD 21817. 2 rooms.

My Fair Lady Inn (1-800-294-3514), 38 Main St., Crisfield, MD 21817. 5 rooms.

Paddlewheel Motel (410-968-2220), 701 W. Main St., Crisfield, MD 21817. 19 rooms, private baths.

Pines Motel (410-968-0900), N. Somerset Ave., Crisfield, MD 21817. 40 rooms, private baths.

Somers Cove Motel (410-968-1900), Box 387, Norris Dr., Crisfield, MD 21817.

Washington Hotel (410-651-2525), 32 Somerset Ave., Princess Anne, MD 21853.

19-A
Bay to Beach

Part 1: Crisfield to Snow Hill

Distance: *37.5 miles one way*
Terrain: *flat countryside, swamp, and forest*
Location: *Somerset and Worcester Counties, Maryland*
Special features: *Rehoboth, Burgess Farm Museum, Pocomoke City*

The Crisfield to Snow Hill trip is part one of the bay to beach journey that ends at Assateague National Seashore on the Atlantic Ocean. The route begins in Crisfield, a major center for the Maryland seafood industry. I recommend taking the tour during Labor Day weekend, when Crisfield hosts its annual National Hard Crab Derby and Fair. About 10,000 visitors come to see Chesapeake Bay crabs race down a ramp to win prizes for their proud owners. The town and marina are alive with food booths, craft stalls, and amusements.

Crisfield is truly a town built on the shells of crabs and oysters. The tour begins on West Main Street at the town dock, a major connecting point for tours to Smith and Tangier Islands. (See Tours 20 and 21.) Here you can catch the ferries that will take you across the bay. A short distance from the dock are a number of restaurants that can provide you with a nourishing breakfast or lunch prior to your trip. My favorite is the Captain's Galley, whose large window overlooks Tangier Sound of Chesapeake Bay. Once out of Crisfield, you will travel through some of the most beautiful farmland of Somerset County. This portion of the county was heavily settled by Mennonites at the turn of the century and still has a flourishing Mennonite farming community. Mennonite women of this region are well known for their handcrafted quilts. Just outside of the vil-

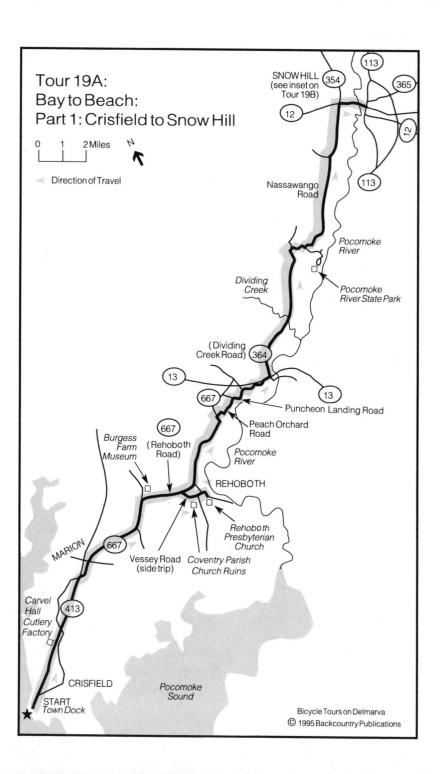

Tour 19A:
Bay to Beach:
Part 1: Crisfield to Snow Hill

0   1   2 Miles

N

◅ Direction of Travel

SNOW HILL
(see inset on
Tour 19B)

113

354

365

12

12

113

Nassawango
Road

Pocomoke
River

Dividing
Creek

Pocomoke
River State Park

(Dividing
Creek Road)   364

13

667   13

Puncheon Landing Road

Peach Orchard
Road

667

(Rehoboth
Road)

Pocomoke
River

Burgess
Farm
Museum

REHOBOTH

667

MARION

Rehoboth
Presbyterian
Church

Vessey Road
(side trip)

Coventry Parish
Church Ruins

Carvel
Hall
Cutlery
Factory

413

CRISFIELD

Pocomoke
Sound

START
Town Dock

★

Bicycle Tours on Delmarva
© 1995 Backcountry Publications

lage of Marion is the county's most interesting collection of Americana, the Burgess Farm Museum, an idiosyncratic, family-owned collection of farm implements and antiques.

Continuing onward, you will come to a half-mile side trip to Rehoboth, and it is well worth taking. Here you can see the Pocomoke River, the early river highway that the colonists used to settle here in the 17th century. The village gets its name from the Bible: Rehoboth means "there is room."

After crossing US 13, you will enter the Pocomoke Forest. Until the Civil War and the coming of the railroad, this was the densest wilderness of Chesapeake Bay country. Timber cutters and shingle makers thrived here; its forests, swamps, and bogs discouraged travelers. Your tour will take you through one of the denser areas of the Pocomoke Forest, and it is essential that you follow directions carefully to avoid getting lost on the myriad country roads that bisect it. While in the forest, you can visit the Nassawango Iron Furnace. (See Tour 22.)

The tour ends at Snow Hill, the county seat of Worcester County. There are two good restaurants in this town. For lunch, try the Judge's Bench. The Snow Hill Inn serves dinners that will ease a tired biker's appetite. Here too you will have a chance to stay at one of the best bed & breakfast inns in Chesapeake country: The River House Inn of Snow Hill, located at Market and Green Streets, is a splendidly furnished Victorian mansion. Its back lawn and gardens roll down to the Pocomoke River, and the house has porches and nooks that offer a serene and private rest. By prior arrangement, evening meals can be served. This inn is a favorite with cross-country bikers, so book your weekend well in advance.

This tour requires a car shuttle from either Snow Hill or Assateague.

Directions for the Ride

0.0 *Our trip begins at the Crisfield town dock.*

The dock is well known for its "liar's benches," where locals tell tall tales to gullible tourists and try to better their friends' outrageous stories.

Proceed out of town on MD 413.

2.4 *Carvel Hall Cutlery Factory.*

There is an outlet store here for locally made cutlery. During

World War II this factory produced the lion's share of machetes used by American soldiers in the Pacific theater.

6.0 *Turn right onto MD 667 and toward US 13 and Pocomoke City.*

6.2 *Village of Marion.*

From 1920 to 1940 this region was the strawberry capital of the East Coast. Every year trainloads of strawberries were harvested on local farms. Now the village is sadly down at the heels.

Continue on MD 667.

9.0 *Turn right on Rehoboth Road/MD 667 and follow signs that point toward US 13. Here you will encounter the Burgess Farm Museum.*

9.6 *SIDE TRIP: Turn right on Vessey Road for the 0.5 mile side trip to Rehoboth, the ruins of Coventry Parish Church, and Rehoboth Presbyterian Church.*

The village is a good place to have a picnic lunch. On your left, as you enter Rehoboth, will be the ruins of Coventry Parish Church, a brick edifice built before the American Revolution; it was subsequently destroyed by Somerset patriots who viewed the Anglican Church as a symbol of England's repressive rule.

Further upriver and within view of Coventry Parish Church is Rehoboth Presbyterian Church. Built in 1705, Rehoboth Presbyterian is notable as the oldest house of worship in the United States used exclusively by the Presbyterian faith. The church was founded by Reverend Francis Makemie, the Scottish parson who spread the Presbyterian faith in the Chesapeake region at the beginning of the 18th century. The church is known for its Flemish-bond brickwork. Its stained-glass windows are a late Victorian addition.

Return to Rehoboth Road/MD 667.

19.0 *Turn right onto Peach Orchard Road toward Pocomoke City. This is an important turn: If you miss it, you will end up on US 13 with nowhere to go!*

20.0 *Turn right on Puncheon Landing Road/Peach Orchard Road.*

21.5 *Turn right on US 13. You will have to cycle a short distance on*

this highway in order to get to Dividing Creek Road. This is the only way to cross the marsh and railroad tracks.

22.2 *Turn left on MD 364 North/Dividing Creek Road.*

27.6 *Dividing Creek Road leads into Nassawango Road. Continue on Nassawango Road.*

28.7 *Entrance to Pocomoke River State Park at Milburn Landing.*

This park is located on a delightful stretch of the Pocomoke River and has picnic facilities, rain shelters, and fresh water. Camping facilities are available, but no swimming is allowed.

35.5 *Turn right on MD 12 and proceed into the town of Snow Hill.*

The architecture of Snow Hill is a feast for the eyes. Cycle down Federal Street, which runs parallel to Market Street. Here you will see a number of Federal-era houses (circa 1814) like Widehaul and Chanceford Hall (now a bed & breakfast). A privately owed home at 109 Federal Street is particularly well known for its cornices and outside chimneys.

Bicycle Repair Services

None on this route.

Attractions

Julia A. Purnell Museum (410-632-0515), 208 W. Market St., Snow Hill, MD. Local history of Snow Hill and Worcester County. Good Victorian-era collection. Weekdays 10–4, weekends 1–4.

Lodging

Chanceford Hall B&B (410-632-2231), 209 W. Federal St., Snow Hill, MD 21863. 5 rooms, private baths, expensive.

River House Inn (410-632-2722), 201 E. Market St., Snow Hill, MD 21863. 9 rooms, private baths, moderate rates.

Snow Hill Inn (410-632-2102), 104 E. Main St., Snow Hill, MD 21863. 4 rooms, private baths, budget rates.

19-B
Bay to Beach

Part 2: Snow Hill to Assateague

Distance: *29 miles one way*
Terrain: *Rolling countryside, beaches*
Location: *Worcester County, Maryland*
Special features: *Assateague National Seashore Park*

This trip will take you across the rolling countryside of Worcester County. As the ride is virtually treeless, I recommend that you use caution during the hot, sunny days of July and August. There is also little shade at the beach. Over-enthusiastic cyclists can suffer heat exhaustion.

The tour is the best and most direct route to Assateague National Seashore Park, a long sandy barrier island jointly administered by the states of Maryland and Virginia and the federal government. It is home to wild ponies, eagles, and a wide variety of other wildlife. Behind the sand dunes of Assateague, the island's forests and marshes invite exploration. The surf is mild here and excellent for swimming. The last leg of the trip takes you to the Barrier Island Visitor Center, where you can obtain plenty of information about the park. There is a $2 admission fee for individuals on bicycles.

The state of Maryland operates a campground at Assateague on a first-come, first-served basis. Campsites at the federally administered campground may be booked in advance.

Caution: To get to the park you must cross over Chincoteague Bay on the Verrazano Bridge. Park rangers *strongly* recommend that you walk your bike across. Drivers are sometimes too busy gawking at the sights to pay heed to cyclists.

Assateague also offers you an excellent opportunity to combine your cycle trip with some backpacking. Follow the 3.5-mile bike trail from Bayberry Drive. There is a hiker campsite at milepost 4 down the beach; proceed on foot. To hike into the backcountry, you need a park permit.

Directions for the Ride

0.0 *Begin your trip in Snow Hill, Maryland, at the Worcester County Library parking area. Proceed on Snow Hill Road/MD 12 out of town heading northwest toward Salisbury.*

1.5 *Turn right onto MD 354 North.*

8.2 *Enter Wicomico County and the hamlet of Whiton.*

11.1 *Turn right onto MD 374, which is the Libertytown and Berlin Road.*

16.5 *Enter Libertytown.*

20.9 *Enter Berlin. Once in Berlin, continue straight. Look for Bay Street. It is a bit tricky. Bay Street is between Farlow's Pharmacy and the local bank. It winds around past the Holland House Bed and Breakfast.*

Berlin is becoming known for its antiques shops and art galleries. You may wish to stop for a cool drink at the Atlantic Hotel's Victorian-style pub. Berlin (accent on the first syllable) is an architectural delight. Its buildings range from the Federal period to the Victorian. Magnolias and ginkgo trees add to the beauty of Berlin's streets. For history buffs, Berlin was the birthplace of Commodore Stephen Decatur (1779–1820), the famous 19th-century naval hero.

22.1 *Cross US 113 and continue on MD 374 to Assateague.*

25.0 *Turn right on MD 611.*

This is your last chance to get water and cool drinks at country stores before Assateague Island.

28.0 *Barrier Island Visitor Center.*

Stop here for tourist and camping information. Prepare to cross Verrazano Bridge.

29.0 *Assateague National Seashore. Turn right and follow signs to*

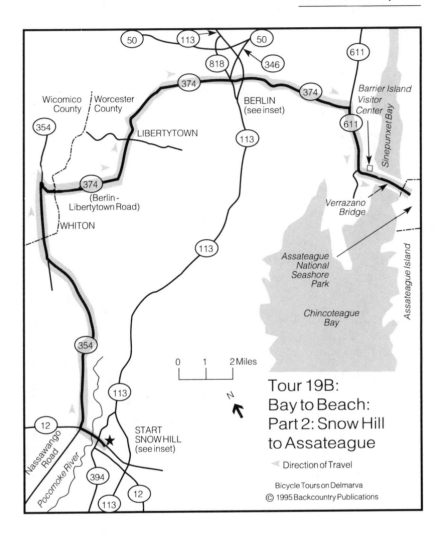

Tour 19B:
Bay to Beach:
Part 2: Snow Hill
to Assateague

◁ Direction of Travel

Bicycle Tours on Delmarva
© 1995 Backcountry Publications

the campground and registration office.

The park serves as a large wildlife refuge for wintering waterfowl populations. The piping plover, a threatened species, nests here at Assateague. You can watch terns and gulls dive for fish, and sandpipers work the beaches and mudflats. Two herds of wild ponies make their homes on Assateague Island as well; on the Maryland side of the park, the ponies are often seen near the campgrounds.

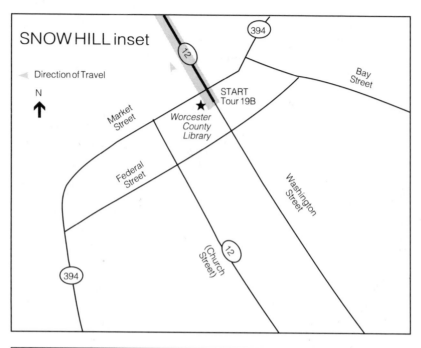

SNOW HILL inset

◄ Direction of Travel

N ↑

(394)
(12)
Bay Street
START Tour 19B
Market Street
★ Worcester County Library
Federal Street
Washington Street
(12) (Church Street)
(394)

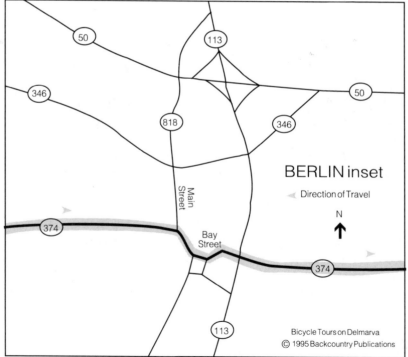

(50)
(113)
(346)
(50)
(818)
(346)

BERLIN inset

◄ Direction of Travel

N ↑

Main Street

(374)
Bay Street
(374)
(113)

Bicycle Tours on Delmarva
© 1995 Backcountry Publications

Bicycle Repair Services

None on this route.

Attractions

Assateague National Seashore Park. The National Park Service offers guided walks that incude examination of Assateague bird life, beaches, salt marshes, dunes, and the bay. Clamming, crabbing, and canoe trips are available.

Taylor House Museum (410-641-1019), 208 N. Main St., Berlin, MD. This large Federal-style building is now the town museum filled with 19th-century Americana. Open Friday and Saturday 1–5.

Lodging

The Atlantic Hotel (410-641-3589), 2 N. Main St., Berlin, MD 21811. 126 rooms, private baths, moderate rates.

Holland House Bed and Breakfast (410-641-1956), 5 Bay St., Berlin, MD 21811. 5 rooms, private baths, moderate rates.

Campsites

Assateague National Seashore Park, under the National Park Service, uses the MISTIX Corporation's reservation system for its campsites. The camping fee is $10 per site. For reservations call 1-800-365-2267 and be prepared to enter the first four letters of the park—ASSA. Have your credit card ready too.

Assateague State Park (410-641-2120) has 311 campsites that feature hot water and flush toilets. The fee is $20 per night on a first-come, first-served basis.

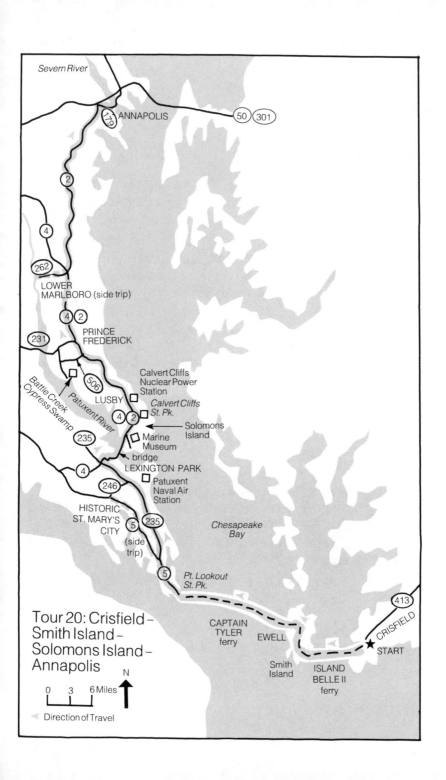

Severn River

179 ANNAPOLIS   50 301

2

4

262

LOWER
MARLBORO (side trip)

4 2

231   PRINCE
              FREDERICK

□   Calvert Cliffs
      506   Nuclear Power
                     Station
Battle Creek
Cypress Swamp   LUSBY   □
                              Calvert Cliffs
              4 2   *St. Pk.*
Patuxent River   ← Solomons
     235   Island

              □ Marine
                 Museum
              bridge
     4   LEXINGTON PARK
     246   □ Patuxent
                 Naval Air
                 Station
HISTORIC   *Chesapeake
ST. MARY'S   Bay*
CITY   5 235
       (side
       trip)
          5
              *Pt. Lookout
               St. Pk.*   413
                                      CRISFIELD
Tour 20: Crisfield–   CAPTAIN   ★ START
Smith Island–   TYLER   EWELL
Solomons Island–   ferry
Annapolis   N   Smith   ISLAND
                         Island   BELLE II
0   3   6 Miles   ferry

◄ Direction of Travel

20
Crisfield–Smith Island–
Solomons Island–Annapolis

Distance: *30 nautical miles, 86 land miles, one way*
Terrain: *Flat to rolling countryside*
Location: *Somerset, St. Mary's, Calvert, Dorchester, and Anne Arundel Counties, Maryland*
Special features: *Smith Island, Chesapeake Bay ferries, Point Lookout, Solomons Island*

Chesapeake excursion ferries make it possible for cyclists to take a land and water tour across the bay to Smith Island, Point Lookout, and Solomons Island. As you travel by boat, you will see the region as watermen see it. After your ferry ride, you can explore Calvert, St. Mary's, and Anne Arundel Counties. You can continue all the way to Annapolis, a good day's ride north of Solomons Island on MD 2.

On this tour, you will be taking two ferries: the *Island Belle II* out of Crisfield for Smith Island, and the *Captain Tyler* from Smith Island for Point Lookout on Chesapeake's western shore. (There is an alternative to the *Island Belle*—if you don't mind having your bike lashed to the top of a small craft. A cheaper mail boat departs Crisfield for Smith Island, usually before 10 AM.) Figure on ferry fees of $8 per person. The *Captain Tyler* charges an additional $2.50 for each bicycle. Please note that you can make this trip only during the tourist season from May through October.

Captain Tyler, Allen Tyler, Captain
Runs Memorial Day through September 30
Ewell, Smith Island, to Point Lookout
Daily: 2 PM (410-425-2771)

Island Belle II
(See introduction for schedule.)

Directions for the Ride

0.0 *Town dock at Crisfield.*

This spot is always abuzz with activity in the late morning. The 50-passenger mail boat, the *Island Belle II,* is being loaded with groceries and other necessities, and you may find your bike lashed on deck to an old refrigerator. The boat is often crammed to the gills with freight boxes, groceries, and passengers. Captain Otis Tyler oversees the loading of the *Island Belle II* and pays for all the provisions from a huge cash roll. (That's the way business is done out on the bay! Watermen don't have much use for checks and credit cards, though they'll trust your word.)

The Island Belle II *leaves the dock promptly at 12:30 PM for Smith Island. On a "slick calm" day the ferry ride to the island takes 40 minutes.*

When the boat arrives at Ewell on Smith Island, check at the dock to learn where the *Captain Tyler* is moored. The boat originates from Point Lookout and usually departs at 2 PM with a boatload of holiday excursionists from the western shore.

Before you depart for Point Lookout you will have about a 40-minute wait, which is ample time to stretch your legs with a ride around Smith Island.

Smith Islanders are almost entirely of British ancestry, and their dialect may be a bit hard to understand. Everyone here depends on the Chesapeake Bay for his or her livelihood, and you will see plenty of boat traffic at the Ewell harbor. Named for Captain John Smith, who sailed the Chesapeake in 1608, Smith Island has a population of about 750—mostly stout, God-fearing Methodists. The Ewell Methodist Church is the central part of island life. There are no bars or taverns on this island.

Despite the difficulties of wresting a living from the Chesapeake Bay, islanders resist the attractions of the mainland economy. The only concession they make is to send their children to high school every day in Crisfield on a high-speed school boat.

At 2 PM the Captain Tyler *whistles its impending departure, and you better scramble aboard quickly for the 2-hour ride to

The mail boat *Island Belle II* at the Crisfield dock
(photo by Orlando V. Wootten)

*Point Lookout on the western shore. The boat will dock at
Point Lookout State Park usually between 3:30 and 4 PM. The
one drawback to the timing of this ride is that you will have to
bicycle through busy Lexington Park, Maryland, at the height
of the rush hour.*

0.0 Point Lookout State Park.

A lovely state park that offers vistas of the bay, camping, and picnic facilities, Point Lookout State Park was tailormade for bikers
on a budget. There is a camp store at the marina and ample tent
sites for weary cyclists who do not wish to push on to Solomons
Island in the late afternoon.

During the Civil War, this area was the site of the notorious
Point Lookout Confederate prisoner of war camp. Many rebel
prisoners of war perished here of malnutrition and the harsh envi-
ronment. Point Lookout Camp was known as the Andersonville of
the North. There is a Confederate cemetery and monument just
outside the park.

From the wharf at Point Lookout State Park, turn left out of the boat ramp and parking lot.

1.9   Turn left onto MD 5.

6.0   Turn right on MD 235.

SIDE TRIP: If you wish to go to Historic St. Mary's City, continue north on MD 5.

Three and a half centuries ago, 140 English settlers came here to begin the Maryland colony for Lord Baltimore. Today the state maintains an 850-acre outdoor museum dedicated to the early 17th-century origins of the state. A replica of the *Dove*, one of sailing vessels that carried settlers from England to the Chesapeake in the 17th century, is moored here.

16.0   *Patuxent Naval Air Station.*

Traffic in the vicinity of this sprawling military base can be quite busy. You will pass the base on your right. Keep well to the right on this highway.

18.2   *Lexington Park.*

Formerly a sleepy crossroads village, Lexington Park now caters to the needs of the large military base. There are plenty of markets and convenience stores here. The rush-hour traffic seems odd when you consider that you are still in a rural area far removed from Washington and Annapolis. Everyone in Lexington Park seems to work at the base, and they are anxious to get home at quitting time.

At the junction of MD 246 and MD 235, continue on MD 235.

22.8   Turn right on MD 4 North.

25.0   *Patuxent River Bridge.*

Because of the rush-hour traffic, I found crossing the bridge an ordeal. The bridge is steep and requires hard pedaling. From the crest of the bridge on a clear day you can see Hoopers Island, so be advised that the bridge is not for the fainthearted. Also, after the crest of the bridge, resist the urge to go hell-for-leather downhill. There are some nasty ruts in the asphalt at the bottom of the bridge, so be careful.

26.5   *Enter Solomons Island.*

The island is well worth the aggravation of the Patuxent River Bridge. Formerly a large fishing and oystering community, Solomons Island is now the sailing mecca of Maryland and the unofficial headquarters of Chesapeake yachtsmen. The community is named for Isaac Solomon, a Civil War–era oyster broker who operated a seafood cannery here. On the Patuxent side of the island is one of the great harbors of the East Coast. The harbor is 2 miles wide and in places over 100 feet deep. Small wonder that Solomons is the darling port of the yachting crowd.

Although Solomons Island receives a heavy influx of tourists in the summer, it does not appeal to the beach crowd. Both visitors and residents alike are affluent and well traveled. Although there are many good restaurants and interesting shops, you will find little resort glitz here.

Solomons is home to the charming and widely known Calvert Marine Museum. There are exhibits on local maritime history, estuarine biology, fossils from Calvert Cliffs, and a circa-1883 lighthouse. During the summer you can take a cruise on a converted bugeye oyster boat.

The Run up to Annapolis

From Solomons Island the trip north to Annapolis is a good day's cycling of 56.8 miles. Should you be interested in spending more time in Calvert County, you can break your journey at mile 28.0 with an overnight in Prince Frederick.

0.0 *Leave Solomons Island.*

In the early morning there will be a significant amount of auto traffic in Solomons as anglers and weekend yachters descend on the port.

6.0 *Just before entering Lusby you will see the signs for Calvert Cliffs State Park on your right.*

In addition to its majestic cliffside view of the Chesapeake Bay, the park is in dinosaur country. Many prehistoric fossils and dinosaur bones have been unearthed in the sandy cliffs by local archaeologists. The bluffs are up to 150 feet high and extend in an arc along the bay for 30 miles. If you walk on the beach you may be lucky enough to find an arrowhead or an old shark's tooth. You can also cycle to the Calvert Cliffs Nuclear Power Station Visitors Center at Lusby, Maryland, which is open daily 10–4.

28.0 Enter Prince Frederick, the seat of Calvert County.

Calvert County is in the midst of an unprecedented period of growth as Washington, D.C., commuters venture deep into southern Maryland in search of the good life and real estate. Unfortunately, much of the old Colonial architecture in the town was destroyed when the British raided Prince Frederick during the War of 1812.

If you are spending the night in Prince Frederick, plan on visiting the Battle Creek Cypress Swamp, the most northern stand of bald cypress trees in America and a national landmark. Footpaths penetrate deep into the swamp. It is 3 miles south of Prince Frederick on MD 506.

37.2 SIDE TRIP: There is an interesting 4.4-mile side trip to Lower Marlboro on the Patuxent River here. Turn left on MD 262. One of the oldest villages in Maryland, Lower Marlboro was a port of entry for tobacco ships in Maryland in 1706; now it is a unique community of restored Colonial homes.

56.8 Continue on MD 2 across the Severn River into Annapolis.

Bicycle Repair Service

Mike's Bikes (410-863-7887), 447-C Great Mills Rd., Lexington Park, MD.

Attractions

The park, museum, and visitors center of Historic St. Mary's City are open daily to the public from 10–5. For further information, write to Historic St. Mary's City, PO Box 39, St. Mary's City, MD 20686.

Calvert Marine Museum (410-326-2042), Solomons Island, MD 20688. Open daily 10–5.

Lodging

Back Creek Inn Bed and Breakfast (410-326-2022), A and Calvert Sts., Solomons, MD 20688. 7 rooms, private baths.

Comfort Inn (410-326-6303), Solomons, MD 20688. 60 rooms.

Harbor View Boat and Breakfast (410-268-9330), 980 Awald Dr., Annapolis, MD 21403.

Hutchins Heritage B&B (410-535-1759), 2860 Adelina Rd., Prince Frederick, MD 20678. 2 rooms, private baths.

Island Manor Motel (410-326-3700), 1 Main St., Solomons, MD 20688.

Note: Because of tourist pressure on Annapolis, book ahead. You may wish to reserve accommodations in Annapolis through Amanda's Bed and Breakfast Reservation Service, 1-800-899-7533.

Campsites

Point Lookout State Park (410-872-5688), PO Box 48, Scotland, MD 20687. Point Lookout is historically important as the site of a notorious Civil War prison camp for Confederate soldiers. It has been called the Andersonville of the North because of the large number of soldiers who died there. There is a beach, camp store, bike trail, fishing pier, and small café.

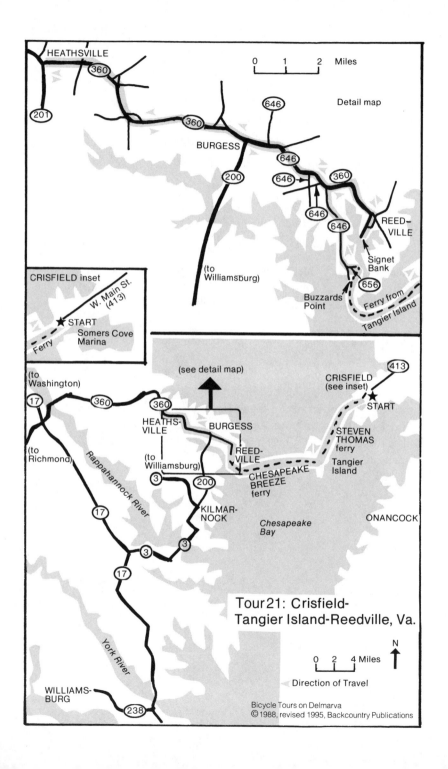

HEATHSVILLE

360

201

360

646 Detail map

BURGESS

646

200

646 646 360

646

REED-
VILLE

656 Signet
Bank

(to
Williamsburg)

Buzzards
Point

Ferry from
Tangier Island

0   1   2   Miles

CRISFIELD inset

W. Main St.
(413)

START
Somers Cove
Marina

Ferry

(to
Washington)

17

360

360

CRISFIELD
(see inset)

413

HEATHS-
VILLE

BURGESS

START

(to
Williamsburg)

REED-
VILLE

STEVEN
THOMAS
ferry

(see detail map)

(to
Richmond)

Rappahannock River

3

200

CHESAPEAKE
BREEZE
ferry

Tangier
Island

17

KILMAR-
NOCK

3

Chesapeake
Bay

ONANCOCK

3

17

York River

WILLIAMS-
BURG

238

Tour 21: Crisfield-
Tangier Island-Reedville, Va.

N

0   2   4 Miles

Direction of Travel

Bicycle Tours on Delmarva
© 1988, revised 1995, Backcountry Publications

21

Crisfield–Tangier Island–Reedville, Virginia

Distance: *34 nautical miles, 29 land miles*
Terrain: *Chesapeake Bay, rolling countryside*
Location: *Somerset County, Maryland, and Northumberland County, Virginia*
Special features: *Ferry crossing of Chesapeake Bay, Tangier Island, Northern Neck of Virginia, side trip to Williamsburg*

This tour combines cycling with a boat excursion across the Chesapeake Bay. The advent of tourism has sparked a salutary development in the bay country—the renewal of ferry excursions on the Chesapeake. It is now possible to cross the bay from either Onancock, Virginia, or Crisfield, Maryland, via Tangier Island and arrive at the western shore of the Chesapeake in Virginia. However, service is seasonal, so plan this tour between Memorial Day and Labor Day. Sometimes the ferry continues into the fall while the weather is good, but it is chancy at best after September 15.

This combined land and water route is excellent for cyclists who have never before seen the Chesapeake Bay in all of its summer splendor. Ospreys nest on buoy lights, and at times swarms of dolphins and bluefish slice through the water. Out in the bay's main channel, ocean-going vessels ply the main route from Norfolk to Baltimore.

Tangier Island remains an intriguing Methodist stronghold of sturdy seafaring families whose language and way of life have hardly changed over the centuries. Men harvest blue crabs and tithe weekly to their church.

The Northern Neck district of Virginia is one of the most isolated and rural regions of the state. Although Northumberland County is less than 70 miles from Richmond, it still retains the remoteness and provinciality of the South as it was in the 1930s. This is one of the few areas that has not been contaminated by the neon, fast-food culture that has disrupted many towns and villages on the Chesapeake.

This tour opens extended possibilities for travel in Virginia as Colonial Williamsburg, Richmond, and Washington are easily accessible to seasoned bikers.

Directions for the Ride

0.0   *Town dock, Crisfield, Maryland. The best strategy is to park your car in the Somers Cove Marina parking lot or on one of the side streets, if you plan to return via the same route. The boat for Tangier Island, the* **Steven Thomas,** *leaves the wharf at 10th Street every day at 12:30 PM. The crew of the* **Steven Thomas** *is experienced in dealing with cyclists, and your bicycle will be stowed safely and securely. It is about 16 nautical miles from Crisfield to Tangier Island.*

16.0 *Tangier Island.*

Tangier is a self-sufficient island of crabbers and fishermen. It has a small airstrip, and its school offers public education from the 1st through the 12th grade. The school population of 115 makes it one of the smallest in the state, but education is held in high esteem among the 750 islanders, and many graduates of the island school have gone on to make their mark in Virginia society. Tangier is a conservative Methodist community, and there are no bars or cocktail lounges on the island.

Tangier Island is a delight for both the novice and the experienced cyclist. There are no cars on the island, and the only traffic consists of other bikes and a small fleet of golf carts used for sightseeing.

The main path consists of a 2.5-mile loop around the island past the neatly kept and prosperous homes of watermen. Tangier can be easily explored in a few hours.

As you cycle through Tangier, notice one of the intriguing features of the island—the individual cemeteries in the front yards of many homes. As the water table is quite high, the graves are covered with heavy cement slabs to prevent tidal water pressure from forcing burial vaults to the surface.

Tangier is well known for its home-cooked seafood dinners, and at Hilda Crockett's Chesapeake House the family-style dinners are "all you can eat." Many tourists are overwhelmed by the abundant meals. After lunch there is time to visit one of the numerous soft-crab shanties and watch watermen separate and box for market soft crabs, which have lost their shells and can be eaten whole.

At 4 PM the excursion boat **Chesapeake Breeze** *departs Tangier Island for Reedville, Virginia. After a crew member stows your bike, the purser will sell you a one-way ticket for $9. The trip to Reedville is 18 nautical miles.*

34.0 *Enter the port of Reedville.*

As you enter Reedville, you will see numerous estates and fine homes near the water's edge. Flocks of ducks and seagulls and boats bobbing gently in the water make Reedville a charming Chesapeake scene. Occasionally, the smell of a nearby fish processing plant is a bit disturbing, however. Reedville is the home port of the Chesapeake Bay menhaden fleet. Most of the fish caught by this fleet is processed for cat food or made into fertilizer.

The **Chesapeake Breeze** *docks at Buzzard's Point, and here you will find a picnic area with an excellent waterfront view. From Buzzard's Point, the land portion of our trip begins.*

0.0 *Buzzard's Point. Take VA 656 0.5 mile to VA 646. Turn right on VA 646.*

1.9 *Turn right on US 360 to Reedville.*

4.0 *Enter Reedville.*

A small Victorian town, Reedville in the past was known as the home of Chesapeake Bay pilots and boat captains. Many were quite prosperous and built solid, imposing homes that can be seen at considerable distances out on the bay. The homes have large porches and backyards that slope toward deep creeks. In Reedville nearly everyone has a boat moored at a pier jutting out from the backyard.

5.0 *The highway dead-ends at a seafood-packing house and the*

Signet Bank. Many residents go out on the water early in the morning so the streets of this town are usually deserted by sunset. People lead a quiet life in Northumberland County. At the Signet Bank, turn around and head north on US 360.

11.2 *Enter the village of Burgess.*

SIDE TRIP: From Burgess you can make a 90-mile overnight side trip to Williamsburg.

To go to Williamsburg, turn left on VA 200, then pick up VA 3 at Kilmarnock. Proceed to the Rappahannock River Bridge. From the bridge continue south on VA 3 to US 17. US 17 is a four-lane highway that should be used with caution. It will take you to VA 238, the Colonial Parkway that leads to Williamsburg.

19.6 *Continuing on US 360, enter Heathsville, the county seat of Northumberland County.*

Heathsville is a quiet antebellum village that still remembers its Confederate dead. Walk around the courthouse grounds and pay special attention to the ruined building behind the courthouse that was once the lawyers row and center of town business life. Heathsville is so quiet that it is hard to believe that it is nearly within automobile commuting distance of Richmond. But then, that is life on the farms and in the villages of the Northern Neck of Virginia—quiet, very quiet.

A Note for the Return Ride

Retrace your steps south on US 360 to Reedville. Two miles out of Reedville is the Bay Motel, the area's only motel. Spend the night here if you wish to take the Chesapeake Breeze back to Tangier Island. The boat departs Buzzard's Point at 10 AM. The area's only restaurant, the Tripp-A-Lee, is 1 mile from the Bay Motel and opens for breakfast at 5 AM. The restaurant is 2 miles from Buzzard's Point, and it is an easy jaunt through cornfield-lined highway to the boat.

Bicycle Repair Services

None on this route.

Lodging

Chesapeake House (804-891-2331), Tangier, VA 23440. Open April 15 through October 15.

Bay Motel (804-453-5171), US 360, Reedville, VA 22539.

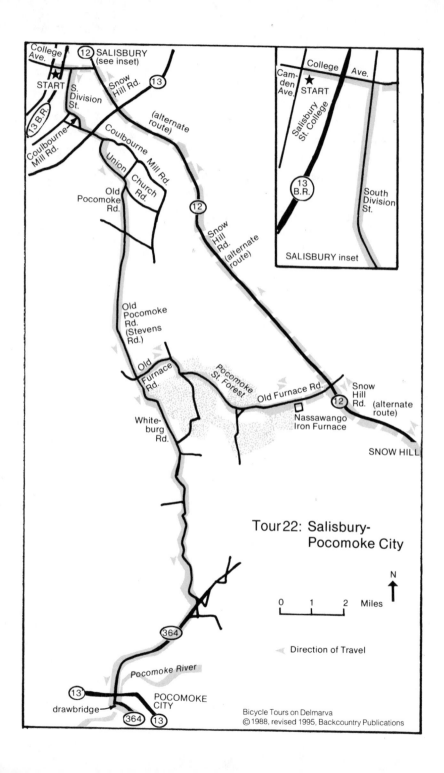

College Ave.

(12) SALISBURY (see inset)

(13)

START

S. Division St.

Snow Hill Rd.

13 B.R.

Coulbourne Mill Rd.

(alternate route)

Coulbourne Mill Rd.

Union Church Rd.

Old Pocomoke Rd.

(12)

Snow Hill Rd. (alternate route)

Old Pocomoke Rd. (Stevens Rd.)

Old Furnace Rd.

Pocomoke St. Forest

Old Furnace Rd.

Snow Hill Rd. (alternate route)

White- burg Rd.

Nassawango Iron Furnace

(12)

SNOW HILL

Tour 22: Salisbury-Pocomoke City

(364)

N

0   1   2   Miles

Direction of Travel

Pocomoke River

(13)

drawbridge

POCOMOKE CITY

(364) (13)

Bicycle Tours on Delmarva
© 1988, revised 1995, Backcountry Publications

SALISBURY inset

College Ave.

Cam- den Ave.

★ START

Salisbury St. College

13 B.R.

South Division St.

SALISBURY inset

22

Salisbury–Pocomoke City

Distance: 35 miles one way
Terrain: Flat to gently rolling
Location: Wicomico and Worcester Counties, Maryland
Special features: Pocomoke Forest, Nassawango Iron Furnace,
Pocomoke City

A cycle trip to Pocomoke City from Salisbury is a refreshing excursion. The route takes you through the heart of the Pocomoke State Forest on the periphery of the wild cypress swamps of the Pocomoke River. Even in the midst of an Eastern Shore summer, most of the route is cool, protected by a beautiful canopy of forest that bathes the highway in shadows. Those of you who have cycled across the open farmlands of the upper Chesapeake in the summer will greatly appreciate this route.

This route is not a loop, so unless you want to retrace the route on your bike, you will need to arrange transportation back to the starting point from Pocomoke City. (If you wish, you can bike 27.5 miles up US 13 North to Salisbury. The road, though busy, has a large, safe shoulder.)

The forests and swamps of the Pocomoke River have their own illustrious past. Rich in game, they were the haunt of the Nanticoke and Wicomico tribes. Later in the antebellum era, they served as a hideout for runaway slaves. The Pocomoke Swamp sustains many cypress trees and over the centuries has supported local timber industries. Bog iron mined from the swamp was smelted into pig iron at the Nassawango Iron Furnace in the heart of the Pocomoke Forest.

Since colonial times, the Pocomoke River has been an important artery of commerce. It is an exceptionally deep river, and Chesapeake vessels carrying petroleum and fertilizer ply its waters.

On this route you will have an excellent chance to see some of the wildlife of the Eastern Shore. The Pocomoke Forest is full of deer, and the rich bird life makes it a birdwatcher's delight.

Directions for the Ride

0.0   *Start at the intersection of College and Camden Avenues at Salisbury State College. Follow College Avenue east to US 13.*

0.3   *Cross US 13 and head east on College Avenue.*

0.5   *Turn right on South Division Street.*

1.8   *Veer left onto Coulbourne Mill Road off South Division Street.*

3.1   *Turn right on Union Church Road. This will take you past Deer Harbor, an affluent Salisbury subdivision.*

4.7   *Turn right onto Old Pocomoke Road. This will take you down through the Pocomoke Forest and into Worcester County. There are no stores or service stations along this route for the next 30 miles.*

10.7   *At the intersection of Old Pocomoke Road and Old Furnace Road, turn left on Old Furnace Road, which will take you through a portion of the Pocomoke Swamp.*

Although there has been a significant amount of logging in this area, the forest and swamp here are still wild and intriguing.

ALTERNATE ROUTE: If you wish to turn this route into a loop back to Salisbury, continue on Old Furnace Road to MD 12/Snow Hill Road. At the intersection of Old Furnace Road and MD 12 you have two options. You can turn left to Salisbury and finish the loop or else turn right and proceed into Snow Hill.

16.7   *Nassawango Iron Furnace.*

Between 1832 and 1847 the Nassawango Iron Furnace supported a flourishing community of miners, sawyers, colliers, moulders, and laborers who were engaged in mining low-grade bog iron from the Pocomoke Forest and Swamp for the large Nassawango iron smelter. The furnace itself was 35 feet high with hot blast tubes built into the top. During its operation, the furnace was loaded with layers of charcoal, bog iron, and oyster shells until it was filled. When heated to molten level, pure iron was let out at

Nassawango Iron Furnace

the casting hearth and cooled into 2-foot-long bars of pig iron. Boats were then loaded with the iron and floated down the nearby Nassawango Creek and thence down the Pocomoke River to the Chesapeake Bay, Baltimore, and beyond. The furnace ceased operation in 1847 when new types of furnaces using better-quality iron ore forced the little furnace town out of business.

Today you can still see the Nassawango Iron Furnace and walk over the grounds of what was once a 5000-acre mining and smelt-ing operation. A number of 19th-century dwellings have been moved to the grounds, and the area is now a public park and museum with guided tours and an operational blacksmith shop.

22.7 *Retrace your route, returning to the intersection of Old Furnace Road and Old Pocomoke Road. Turn left on Old Pocomoke Road.*

Note: Old Pocomoke Road suffers from several confusing name changes, but it is the only due-south road in the area, so stay on it. At this point Old Pocomoke Road becomes Whiteburg Road.

30.5 *At the end of Old Pocomoke Road/Whiteburg Road, turn right on MD 364.*

33.4 *Dividing Creek Market and Country Store.*

34.8 *There is a traffic light at the intersection of MD 364 and US 13. Cross US 13 and follow MD 364 to the left, crossing the Pocomoke River drawbridge.*

35.2 *Enter Pocomoke City.*

An old river town located about 10 miles from the mouth of the river, Pocomoke City retains its regional flavor and heritage. Though the steamboats that once gave the town its prosperity as a commercial and agricultural entrepôt are long gone, Pocomoke is still a neat and tidy town of small shops, churches, and restau-rants. Explore the town's river walk that runs in an east-west direc-tion immediately after the drawbridge.

There are fast-food restaurants and motels conveniently locat-ed on nearby US 13, which runs parallel to the town's main thor-oughfare. Also, Pocomoke City is an excellent launching site for bike trips either to Snow Hill or Virginia's Eastern Shore.

Bicycle Repair Services

Salisbury Schwinn Cyclery (410-546-4747), 1414 S. Salisbury Blvd., Salisbury, MD.

Attractions

Nassawango Iron Furnace is listed in the National Register of Historic Places and is open April through October. For information, telephone 410-632-2032.

Lodging

Days Inn (410-957-3000), 1540 Ocean Hwy., Pocomoke City, MD 21851.

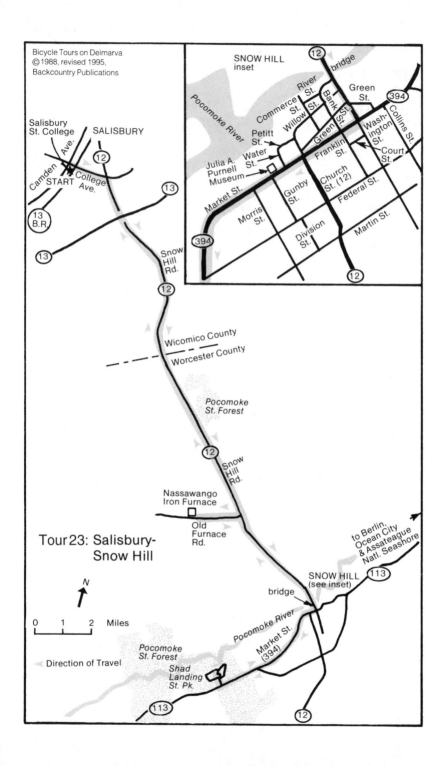

Bicycle Tours on Delmarva
©1988, revised 1995,
Backcountry Publications

SNOW HILL
inset

Pocomoke River

Commerce St.
River St.
Willow St.
Bank St.
Green St.
Green St.
Franklin St.
Washington St.
Collins St.
Court St.
Petitt St.
Water St.
Julia A. Purnell Museum
Market St.
Gunby St.
Church St. (12)
Federal St.
Morris St.
Division St.
Martin St.

bridge

Salisbury St. College
SALISBURY
Camden Ave.
College Ave.
START
Snow Hill Rd.

Wicomico County
Worcester County

Pocomoke St. Forest

Snow Hill Rd.

Nassawango Iron Furnace
Old Furnace Rd.

Tour 23: Salisbury-Snow Hill

N

0   1   2   Miles

Direction of Travel

to Berlin, Ocean City & Assateague Natl. Seashore

SNOW HILL (see inset)

bridge

Pocomoke River
Market St. (394)

Pocomoke St. Forest

Shad Landing St. Pk.

23
Salisbury–Snow Hill

Distance: 18 miles one way
Terrain: Flat to rolling countryside
Location: Wicomico and Worcester Counties, Maryland
Special features: Snow Hill, Shad Landing State Park

The trip to Snow Hill is a perfect cycle outing for those who wish to combine a day of biking with a picnic and a self-guided exploration of a Victorian town and a very popular state park. Also, the bike ride to Snow Hill offers a number of opportunities for the experienced cyclist. You can push on to Chincoteague (see Tour 24) or take the loop down to Nassawango Iron Furnace and either Pocomoke City or Princess Anne (see Tour 22 and Tour 18).

Chartered in 1686, Snow Hill is the county seat of Worcester County and an important regional center. Though the town may give the first-time visitor the impression that this is just another sleepy Eastern Shore town, nothing could be farther from the truth. Snow Hill is an important legal center (all the legal matters of Ocean City must be taken care of here) and a major agricultural town. It is also the gateway for tourism in Worcester County. Snow Hill, for example, is well known as a place for canoeing, picnicking, hiking, bird-watching, and nature walks.

The local architecture of Snow Hill is most impressive, and the Colonial and 19th-century examples are exceptional. Snow Hill's great gem is All Hallows Episcopal Church, which was established in 1692; the present structure was built in 1756. In those days, the cost of construction was measured in pounds of tobacco, and All Hallows cost 80,000 pounds of the "royal weed." You can cycle through the historic district and see many of Snow Hill's fine homes from curbside. Unlike many other areas, everyday people from all walks of life continue to live

The Worcester County Court House in Snow Hill, Maryland
(*photo by Orlando V. Wootten*)

and raise families in these exceptionally fine Colonial and Victorian homes. The town has not yet been gentrified by wealthy outsiders from the western shore.

In the 17th century, Snow Hill was a royal port with direct access to London. The Pocomoke River, with its deep water, easily accommodated colonial oceangoing commerce, and Snow Hill carried on a lively trade with London. After the Revolution, Snow Hill was an important shipbuilding center and steamboat landing. Originally part of Somerset County, Snow Hill became the administrative center of Worcester County when it was formed in 1754.

You will enjoy the quiet, brick-sidewalked and tree-lined streets of Snow Hill. Also, the town has an excellent Victorian restaurant, the Snow Hill Inn, which offers some of the finest Eastern Shore cooking to be found in the region. If you stay overnight at the inn, you will be assured of a sitting at the evening meal, which is by reservation only.

You can get a brochure at the tourist office in the nearby courthouse that describes a walking tour of the town. I recommend the following houses that are well worth seeing on your cycle trip to Snow Hill:

1. Chanceford is a large Federal-period house at 209 Federal Street that was built in 1792 supposedly for Robert Morris, the "financier of the American Revolution." The floors and woodwork are original, and the house has seven working fireplaces.
2. The Teagle-Townsend House at 208 West Federal Street was built around 1814. A great chimney dominates the south end of the house.

While I am not an architectural expert, I have chosen these two houses to whet your appetite to explore Federal Street and other avenues in this historically rich town. By all means, get the walking-tour brochure and embark on an adventure in history.

After you have seen the town and lunched at the Snow Hill Inn, it will be time to press on to Shad Landing State Park. Locals call it Shad Landing, but its official name is Shad Landing Area of Pocomoke River State Park. Shad Landing is one of two separate areas of the state park. Also, what is especially appealing about this cycle route is that the park provides you with opportunities to take either guided canoe trips or self-directed trips through the great Pocomoke Swamp.

This is an easy route; the highway is flat and the way from Salisbury to Snow Hill is well marked, which makes it an excellent tour for the novice cyclist worried about having the physical ability to complete the tour.

This tour is one way, so you should arrange to be met by car or van in Snow Hill if you do not choose to push on to other destinations.

Directions for the Ride

0.0   *The trip begins in Salisbury at the intersection of College and Camden Avenues at the corner of Salisbury State College. As in Tours 14, 16, and 22, we begin here because it is convenient for parking and the outward route offers minimum automobile traffic. Turn right on College Avenue.*

1.4   *Turn right on MD 12/Snow Hill Road. The Holly Center, an institution for developmentally disabled youths, will be on your right.*

7.3   *Worcester County line. The road widens here and you will have a much better shoulder to ride on than you did coming out of Salisbury.*

13.9   *Nassawango Iron Furnace Road.*

If you wish, you can turn right here to go to the Nassawango Iron Furnace museum and park, the site of a great bog iron furnace for smelting iron ore in the 19th century (see Tour 22).

17.9   *Pocomoke River Bridge. Enter Snow Hill.*

Adjacent to this old drawbridge is the Pocomoke River Canoe Company, which rents canoes for exploring the Pocomoke River and its environs. Once out on the river, you will enter the same kind of habitat as did the colonial settlers, and your chances of spotting ospreys, blue herons, egrets, and other wildlife are excellent. The boats come equipped with life vests. The Pocomoke River Canoe Company also conducts group tours of the Pocomoke Swamp, a beautiful primitive tract of white oak, bald cypress, and picturesque water routes.

18.0   *Turn right on Market Street in Snow Hill. This will put you in the center of town. Follow Market Street to the Julia Purnell Museum at 208 West Market Street.*

This museum houses an interesting collection of 19th-century memorabilia. Here you will be able to see Victorian needlework, old farm tools, spinning wheels, kitchen equipment, antique toys, and Native American artifacts. The museum is open weekdays 9–5; weekends 1–5 (410-632-0515).

18.2 *If you wish to continue on to Shad Landing State Park, continue on Market Street out of Snow Hill. Market Street becomes MD 394, which takes you to US 113.*

21.2 *Turn right into Shad Landing State Park.*

This park takes its name from its former use by shad anglers as a harbor and landing on the Pocomoke River. In addition to a large picnic area along the river, the park has a campground. You also can rent canoes and motorboats and travel through a small, well-marked portion of the Pocomoke Swamp. In the late afternoon it is pleasant to ride along the park road down to the river wharf and watch pleasure boats coming up from the Chesapeake to moor for the night. Also, if you camp at Shad Landing, you are permitted to use the park swimming pool.

A Note for the Return Ride

Simply retrace your route back to Snow Hill. If you wish a lengthier trip, you can proceed up US 113, which will take you to Berlin and routes to Assateague National Seashore and Ocean City (see Tour 27).

Bicycle Repair Services

Salisbury Schwinn Cyclery (410-546-4747), 1404 S. Salisbury Blvd. (US 13), Salisbury, MD.

Attractions

The Pocomoke River Canoe Company is open Memorial Day through Labor Day; Barry Laws, proprietor; 410-632-3971.

Lodging

Chanceford Hall B&B (410-632-2231), 201 Federal St., Snow Hill, MD 21863. 5 rooms, private baths.

River House Inn (410-632-2722), 201 E. Market St., Snow Hill, MD 21863.

Snow Hill Inn (410-632-2102), 104 E. Market St., Snow Hill, MD 21863.

Campsites

Shad Landing (410-632-2566), Pocomoke River State Park, Snow Hill, MD 21863. Shad Landing is 4 miles south of Snow Hill on US 113. This 544-acre park on the Pocomoke River is a delightful, relatively insect-free area.

24

Snow Hill, Maryland–Chincoteague, Virginia

Distance: *47 miles one way*
Terrain: *Flat to rolling countryside*
Location: Worcester County, Maryland, and Accomack County, Virginia
Special features: Chincoteague Island, Chincoteague National Wildlife Refuge

This trip should be considered in conjunction with Tours 22 and 23. These three tours make an excellent weekend of cross-country cycling in any season and offer a combination of small towns, historic centers, and scenic natural environments.

There is a certain enchantment about Chincoteague. Perhaps it stems from the romantic tales of lost pirate treasure and herds of wild horses that have roamed on the island since the 16th century. Perhaps it is the golden brown expanses of marsh and wild seashore that form a rare setting in the mid-Atlantic region.

Chincoteague lies just beyond Chincoteague Channel, a large shallow body of water traversed by a narrow strip of highway. Although settlers from the Jamestown colony of Virginia came here over three centuries ago, the town remained an isolated fishing village on a remote island until the state connected it to the mainland with a causeway in 1922.

By any resort standard, Chincoteague Island is small. Its population of 3555 is set in its ways, and islanders are in no hurry to emulate towns to the north like Cape May and Ocean City. The town is a simple village of narrow crisscrossing streets, and the flavor of local life is more of New England than of the South. The houses are simple white clapboard, and there are few bars or resort night spots. On a summer night in Chincoteague, the most exciting places in town are the local ice cream parlors.

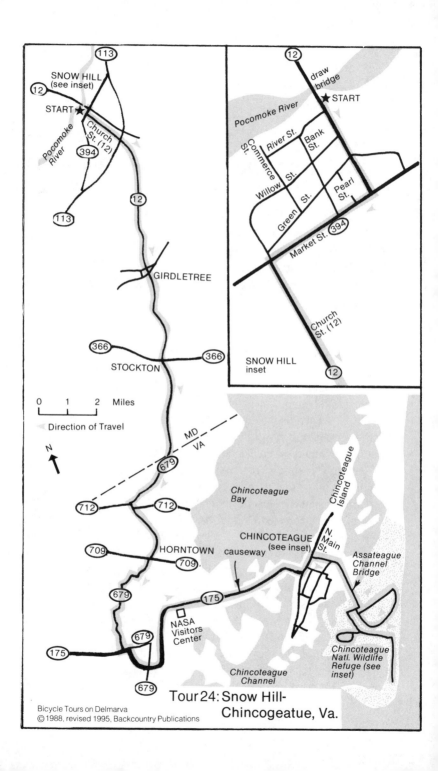

113

SNOW HILL
(see inset)

12

START

Pocomoke
River

Church
St. (12)

394

12

113

GIRDLETREE

366   366

STOCKTON

0   1   2   Miles

Direction of Travel

N

MD
VA

679

712   712

709   HORNTOWN

709

679

175   175

NASA
Visitors
Center

679

175

679

12   draw
          bridge

START

Pocomoke River

Commerce
St.

River St.   Bank
                   St.

Willow
St.

Green   St.   Pearl
          St.   St.

Market St.   394

Church
St. (12)

12

SNOW HILL
inset

Chincoteague
Bay

Chincoteague
Island

CHINCOTEAGUE
(see inset)

N.
Main
St.

causeway

Assateague
Channel
Bridge

Chincoteague
Channel

Chincoteague
Natl. Wildlife
Refuge (see
inset)

Tour 24: Snow Hill-
Chincogeatue, Va.

Bicycle Tours on Delmarva
© 1988, revised 1995, Backcountry Publications

Chincoteague is famous for its salty oysters and seafood, and the town is still the home port of a large commercial fishing fleet. Lately Chincoteague has also become known as the home port for charter boats engaged in shark fishing. This dangerous sport has become popular with affluent tourists, and on the day I cycled to Chincoteague I spotted several large sharks hanging as trophies near one of the boat wharves.

The Chincoteague National Wildlife Refuge is just a short ride out of town. Created in 1943, the refuge has over 9000 acres of land, and within that area are some of the finest stretches of unbroken primal beach, rolling dunes, marshes, and freshwater ponds. The chief citizens of the island are the Chincoteague wild ponies. Though they love to cadge snacks from sympathetic tourists and appear docile, they are wild animals; they can kick and bite, so respect them. In July the Chincoteague Fire Department stages its annual Pony Roundup and Swim. To preserve the ecological balance of the herd, ponies are culled and sold at auction. This popular event attracts thousands of tourists and is fun to see and photograph.

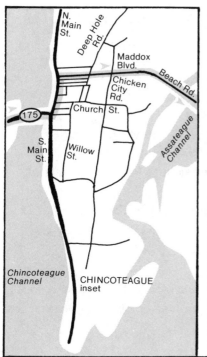

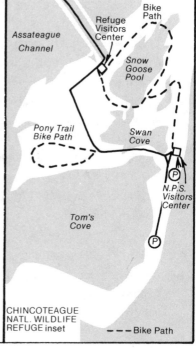

If you want to experience the island as the locals do, come to Chincoteague in the fall after the tourists have gone. There is no hectic rush to get to the beach, and traffic on the causeway to the island is less bothersome.

Native Americans called the island "Gingoteague," "the beautiful land across the water." When you come to Chincoteague you will see that the Native Americans were right.

Directions for the Ride

0.0   *The trip begins at the old drawbridge on MD 12, just as you enter Snow Hill from Salisbury. You will find ample parking for your car on the side streets around the new county library and municipal building (see the map of Snow Hill in Tour 23).*

0.2   *Turn right on Market Street.*

0.3   *Turn left on Church Street/MD 12 and follow the signs for Girdletree and Stockton.*

1.8   *Intersection and stop sign at US 113. Cross US 113 and continue on MD 12.*

6.1   *Enter the village of Girdletree.*

There is a country market that sells cold drinks and snacks.

9.1   *Reach the village of Stockton.*

In this area there is a kosher poultry plant, and tourists are occasionally surprised to see orthodox Jewish butchers from New York City in this remote rural hamlet.

9.6   *Fleming's Grocery and intersection with MD 366. Continue south on MD 12.*

13.0   *Virginia state line. MD 12 becomes VA 679. Continue on VA 679.*

The land becomes more rolling now, and distances between villages and towns are longer.

16.8   *Enter Horntown, Virginia.*

21.0   *At the intersection of VA 679 and VA 175, turn left on VA 175.*

Coffin's Market is a good place to stop for a lunch of homemade sandwiches.

Wild ponies at Chincoteague

24.4 NASA visitors center.

You are now at the NASA/Wallops Facility of the Goddard Space Flight Center. This agency of the National Aeronautics and Space Administration has been here since 1945 and is concerned primarily with tracking space satellites and abating aircraft noise. The Wallops Facility also conducts considerable research in space rocketry. The visitors center, which has many fine displays chronicling the history of space research, is open 5 days a week, Thursday through Monday, 10–4.

29.2 *After crossing the long, narrow causeway across the Chincoteague Channel, enter the town of Chincoteague.*

I left Snow Hill on a July morning at 10 AM and, even with stopping and taking a leisurely pace, I arrived in Chincoteague around 2 PM. As there is much to see in the wildlife refuge, I recommend staying overnight at either a motel or a campground. There are plenty of both in the area.

After you have rested and found a place to stay, cycle out to the refuge; because of the heat, the best times in the summer are in the early morning or late in the afternoon.

At the Chincoteague Channel Bridge, turn left and cycle up North Main Street. Turn right on Maddox Boulevard and proceed 2 miles to the Assateague Channel Bridge.

This is the touristy part of Chincoteague; motels and restaurants have sprung up in abundance in the last few years. Just before the bridge is Tom's Cove Campground, a sprawling park and campground that can get quite crowded in the summer.

Cross the Assateague Channel Bridge and follow the signs to the wildlife refuge bike path on the left.

The bike paths of Chincoteague National Wildlife Refuge are, to put it mildly, wonderful! You can get away from automobile traffic and commune with nature.

The park has two bike loops: The Snow Goose Pool Loop (3.5 miles); and The Pony Trail (1.5 miles).

These loops take you through forest and marsh and along tidewater pools of breathtaking beauty. Just don't daydream too much while you are communing with nature or you may collide with a jogger.

After you do both loops, follow the auto route to the beach.

Go ahead and take a swim. There is a large bathhouse and visitors center at the beach, and there are steel bike racks to secure your bicycle.

After a swim or walk along part of the 12-mile wild beach, return to Chincoteague and splurge at one of the local ice cream parlors.

A Note for the Return Ride

As this tour is not a loop, you should arrange to be picked up by car or van after you have spent one night in Chincoteague. If you have the time and inclination, you may wish to pick up on Tour 26 and proceed to either Wachapreague or Cape Charles.

Bicycle Repair Services

None on this route.

Attractions

According to *Whitelaw's History,* in 1671 the first European laid claim to the island known to Native Americans as "Gingoteague," or "beautiful land across the water."

Assateague Light. This 145-foot lighthouse was constructed in 1857 and still stands guard over the Chincoteague shoals.

Chincoteague oysters and clams constitute the island's main industry. Crabbing is also a popular pastime. The Chincoteague Seafood Festival is held each May. For information and tickets contact: Chincoteague Chamber of Commerce, Box 258, Chincoteague, VA 23336; 804-336-6161.

The Oyster Museum is on Maddox Boulevard. Exhibits, including narrated dioramas, depict the history of oystering in the region from the 1600s to the present. The admission fee is $2.

Chincoteague Pony Roundup and Swim draws several thousand spectators on the last Wednesday and Thursday in July. On these days the wild ponies are rounded up from their home on Assateague Island to swim at low tide across the narrow channel to Chincoteague. The ponies are sold at auction, with the proceeds benefiting the local volunteer fire department. Plan to book your motel accommodations in advance if you want to be in Chincoteague for this event.

Muller's Old Fashioned Ice Cream Parlor, 434 Main St., in the heart of Chincoteague. Have dessert on the candlelit porch on a summer evening.

Lodging

Note: Most of the motels in Chincoteague are located on Maddox Boulevard and are reasonably priced. Some require a reservation deposit in the summer.

Birchwood Motel (804-336-6133), 3650 S. Main St., Chincoteague, VA 23336.

187

Driftwood Manor Lodge (1-800-553-6117), Maddox Blvd. and Beach Rd. (the closest motel to the beach), Chincoteague, VA 23336. 52 rooms, private baths. Pool and outdoor picnic area.

Main Street House Bed and Breakfast (1-800-491-2027), 4356 Main St., Chincoteague, VA 23336.

Miss Molly's B&B (804-336-6686), 4141 Main St., Chincoteague, VA 23336. 7 rooms, 5 with private bath. Full breakfast and traditional English afternoon tea. Marguerite Henry stayed here while writing her book *Misty of Chincoteague.*

Sea Hawk Motel (804-336-6527), 6250 Maddox Blvd., Chincoteague, VA 23336. 28 rooms, private baths; 5 two-bedroom units; 8 apartments with kitchens; and 2 cottages. Inexpensive.

The Watson House Victorian Inn, Bed and Breakfast (804-336-1564), 4240 Main St., Chincoteague, VA 23336. 6 rooms, private baths. Afternoon tea and refreshments. Minimum 2-night stay in the summer.

Author's note: I would be remiss if I did not mention a gem of a restaurant B&B called Garden and the Sea Inn (804-824-0672). The meals here are delightful and served in the tradition of a French country inn. It is located in New Church, Virginia, about 15 minutes north of Chincoteague by car. Reservations strongly encouraged. Open April through October.

Campsites

Tom's Cove Family Campground (804-336-6498), PO Box 122, Chincoteague, VA 23336. Unlike Assateague Park in Maryland, there is no public seashore camping at Chincoteague.

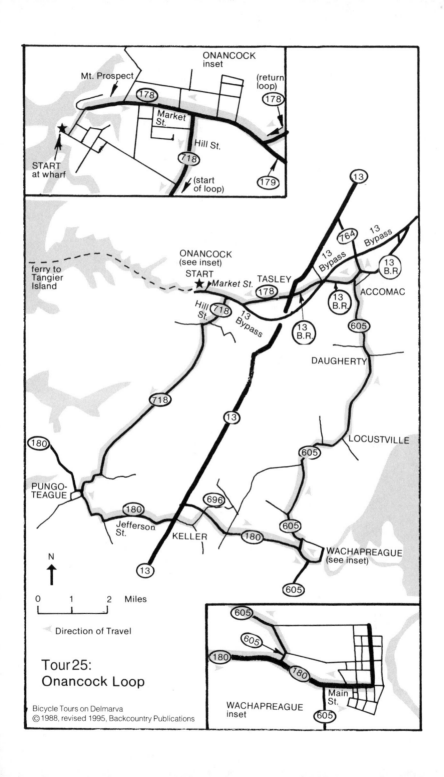

ONANCOCK
inset

Mt. Prospect

178

(return loop)
178

Market St.

Hill St.

718

START at wharf

(start of loop)

179

13

764

13 Bypass

13 Bypass

13 B.R.

ferry to Tangier Island

ONANCOCK (see inset)
START

Market St.
178

TASLEY

ACCOMAC

Hill St.
718

13 Bypass

13 B.R.

13 B.R.

605

DAUGHERTY

718

13

605

LOCUSTVILLE

180

696

PUNGO-TEAGUE

180

605

Jefferson St.

KELLER

180

WACHAPREAGUE (see inset)

N

0   1   2   Miles

605

Direction of Travel

605

605

Tour 25:
Onancock Loop

180

605

180

Main St.

WACHAPREAGUE
inset

Bicycle Tours on Delmarva
© 1988, revised 1995, Backcountry Publications

25

Onancock Loop

Distance: *32.5 miles*
Terrain: *Flat to rolling countryside, strong headwinds in autumn*
Location: *Accomack County, Virginia*
Special features: *Onancock, Wachapreague, Accomac*

The town of Onancock, Virginia, on the Eastern Shore of the Chesapeake, is about 58 miles due south of Salisbury, Maryland. The drive down through Accomack County is worth the trip because you will encounter a 70-mile peninsula that is still unspoiled by tourism and commercial development. The Eastern Shore of Virginia moves at a pace much slower than the rest of Delmarva, and the names on the land—like Pungoteague, Wachapreague, and Modest Town—reflect the quaintness of the region. The two counties of the Virginia Eastern Shore, Accomack and Northampton Counties, are large agricultural regions that encompass some 120,000 acres of cropland. Over 30,000 acres are planted annually in Irish potatoes. Large amounts of peppers, sweet potatoes, tomatoes, and snap beans are also grown.

The Eastern Shore of Virginia is one of the oldest settled regions in America. English colonists came here as early as 1620. Originally, the region was referred to as Accomack Plantation, but by 1663 the two counties had been organized to give better political and economic coherence to the area. The Eastern Shore of Virginia was able to preserve much of its early charm until the opening in 1965 of the Chesapeake Bay Bridge-Tunnel, which connected the region with Norfolk and the rest of the state. Accomack and Northampton Counties then lost their relative isolation.

This tour begins in Onancock with good reason. First there are good overnight accommodations here. Second, you can, if you like, take an excursion boat from the wharf at Onancock to Tangier Island. While the

Francis Makemie Memorial in Accomac, Virginia

ferry schedule is subject to change, you can get ticket and passenger information from the Hopkins Restaurant and General Store at the wharf. Usually in the summer the *Spirit of '76* sails from the wharf for Tangier Island at 10 AM and returns at 1:45 PM. For ticket information call 804-787-8220.

Directions for the Ride

0.0 *The loop begins at the wharf parking lot at Hopkins Restaurant in Onancock.*

Onancock has been settled since the 1650s, and its deepwater harbor makes it an attractive Chesapeake port for ships and yachts of all sizes. Although Onancock has little Colonial architecture, it is a quaint town. To see Onancock at its most charming, take the bridge across the creek at the Onancock wharf and proceed up the hill to Mount Prospect. There you will have an excellent vista of 19th-century houses proudly situated on high banks overlooking the tidewater. It is one of the prettiest waterside residential communities on the Eastern Shore of Virginia.

Proceed up Market Street to the main section of Onancock.

0.4 *The Kerr Place, a plantation built in 1799, will be on your left.*
It is currently the home of the Eastern Shore of Virginia Historical Society and is open to the public daily 10–4.

0.7 *Colonial Manor Inn.*

0.9 *Turn right on Hill Street. A Shore Stop convenience store will be on the right-hand corner. This is the route to Pungoteague.*

2.0 *Turn left on VA 178 to Pungoteague.*

6.3 *South Accomack Elementary School will be on your right.*

7.8 *Site of Fowkes Tavern.*
In 1665, the first recorded play in English America, *The Bear and The Cub*, was performed here.

8.1 *Enter Pungoteague, a small village and crossroads.*

8.4 *Turn left on VA 180 East. Follow the signs for Keller, Virginia. Guy's Convenience Market is at this intersection.*

11.5 *Enter the hamlet of Keller. Turn left on VA 180/Jefferson Street, which ultimately becomes N.R. North Street.*

11.8 *Intersection of VA 180 and US 13. Cross US 13 and go straight ahead onto VA 696/N.R. North Street. Use caution crossing the railroad tracks.*

12.3 *Swing to the left on VA 696.*

12.8 *At the stop sign, turn right on VA 180.*

16.3 *Enter Wachapreague.*
This is strictly a fisherman's town and is home of the largest charter fishing fleet on the Eastern Shore of Virginia. Wachapreague is known for its seatrout and flounder fishing.

16.7 *Proceed into town. At the stop sign, the waterfront and the Island House Restaurant will be straight ahead.*
From here you can proceed to explore this little village. Wachapreague is laid out like a checkerboard, and you can't get lost. Just follow any street to the water. The Wachapreague Marina Restaurant serves hot food at reasonable prices. Rest here awhile before continuing your loop.

16.7 *Go back up Main Street and out of Wachapreague on VA 180.*

17.6 *Turn right on VA 605 for Accomac.*

19.6 *Chancetown, population 11, the smallest hamlet on the Eastern Shore of Virginia.*

22.2 *Locustville and Locustville Academy.*

Built in 1859 as a school for planters' children, the academy has been recently restored as a historic place.

24.2 *Hamlet of Daugherty.*

26.5 *Enter Accomac.*

One of the most charming colonial villages on Virginia's Eastern Shore, Accomac is a photographer's delight. Accomac was settled as early as 1624, and its continuous court records date from 1632. Most of the houses in Accomac have been carefully restored, and there is a kind of 18th-century ambience to the town. The large frame houses with dormer windows and solid multiple chimneys are reminders of Accomac's prosperity as a legal and market center during the antebellum period.

26.7 *At the stop sign turn right on US Business Route 13.*

26.9 *At the intersection of US Business Route 13 and VA 764 turn left. The Accomack County Court House will be on your left.*

27.0 *The Accomac Debtors Prison will be on your right.*

Built in 1784, this prison housed the county jailer and debtors until the Virginia Legislature brought imprisonment for debt absolutely to an end in 1849.

Retrace your route on VA 764 to the courthouse and US Business Route 13. At the intersection of US Business Route 13 and VA 764, continue straight for a minitour of Accomac. You will now be on VA 1502.

27.2 *At the stop sign turn right. The Makemie Presbyterian Church will be on your right.*

27.3 *Proceed 1 block to the stop sign. Turn right on VA 605.*

27.4 *Turn left onto US Business Route 13.*

28.4 Cross US 13 and stay on US Business Route 13. The Whispering Pines Motel will be on your right.

28.9 Enter Tasley.

29.5 At the stop sign, you will be at the intersection of US 13, VA 178, and VA 316. Go straight ahead on VA 178 West.

30.8 Enter Onancock.

30.9 At the stop sign turn right on VA 178 West and continue into Onancock.

32.5 Reach Onancock wharf and Hopkins Restaurant and General Store. Treat yourself to a cold drink, as this is the end of your loop.

Bicycle Repair Services

None on this route.

Lodging

Colonial Manor Inn (804-787-3521), 84 Market St., Onancock, VA 23417.

The Spinning Wheel Bed & Breakfast (804-787-7311), 31 North St., Onancock, VA 23417. 5 rooms, private baths.

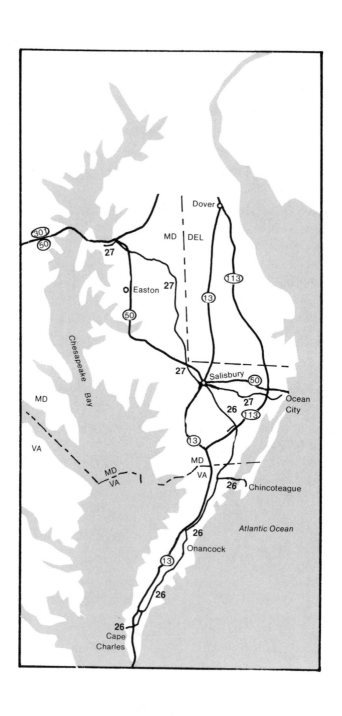

TWO CHESAPEAKE CENTURIES

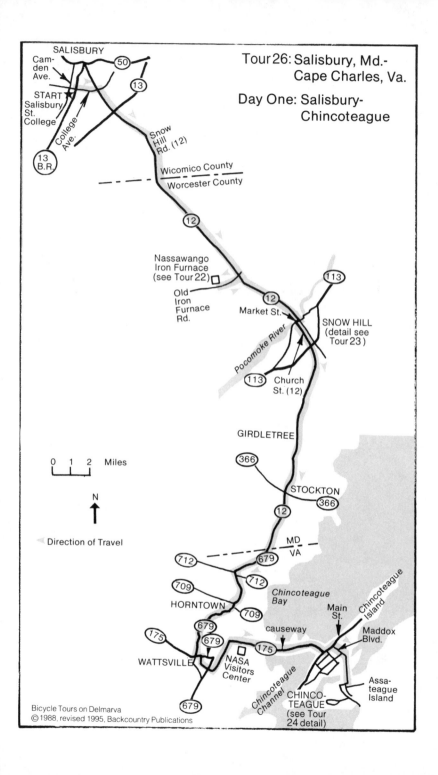

SALISBURY

Camden Ave.

50

13

START
Salisbury
St.
College

College Ave.

13
B.R.

Snow Hill Rd. (12)

Wicomico County
Worcester County

12

Nassawango
Iron Furnace
(see Tour 22)

Old
Iron
Furnace
Rd.

Tour 26: Salisbury, Md.-
Cape Charles, Va.

Day One: Salisbury-
Chincoteague

113

12

Market St.

SNOW HILL
(detail see
Tour 23)

Pocomoke River

113   Church
St. (12)

GIRDLETREE

0   1   2   Miles

N

Direction of Travel

366

STOCKTON
366

12

712

679

MD
VA

712

709

HORNTOWN   709

175   679

679

WATTSVILLE

679

NASA
Visitors
Center

Chincoteague
Bay

causeway

175

Chincoteague Channel

Main
St.

Chincoteague Island

Maddox
Blvd.

Assa-
teague
Island

CHINCO-
TEAGUE
(see Tour
24 detail)

Bicycle Tours on Delmarva
© 1988, revised 1995, Backcountry Publications

26

Salisbury, Maryland–Cape Charles, Virginia

Distance: 125 miles one way
Time and distance planning: 3 days. Salisbury, Maryland, to
 Chincoteague, Virginia: 47 miles; Chincoteague to Wachapreague: 41
 miles; Wachapreague to Cape Charles: 37 miles
Terrain: Flat with occasional hills
Location: Wicomico and Worcester Counties, Maryland; Accomack and
 Northampton Counties, Virginia
Special features: Snow Hill, NASA visitors center, Chincoteague,
 Assateague Island, Wachapreague, Eastville, Cape Charles

This 100-mile-plus tour or century has been designed to introduce the
cyclist to the lower Chesapeake region. Anyone who has an appreciation
of the sea and 18th- and 19th-century architecture will enjoy this fascinating ride. The lower Eastern Shore of Maryland and Virginia is less
commercialized and touristy than the rest of the Delmarva Peninsula,
and it retains a kind of quaint southern charm and architectural distinc-
tiveness that make it a worthwhile tour for the serious biker. This is a
land of small fishing ports and tomato and potato farms. On the lower
Eastern Shore, the Old South is not a memory. It is everyday life for a historically rooted, confident, and gentle people.

With the exception of VA 175 (the causeway to Chincoteague), automobile traffic is very light on the route suggested. I have scheduled 3
days for this tour, with destinations that have motel accommodations.
The distances are deliberately under 50 miles per day because many of
you will be biking this route in the summer. Often during torrid summer
days on the Delmarva Peninsula, 50 miles can seem like 500.

This tour begins at the corner of Camden and College Avenues at the
campus of Salisbury State College in Salisbury. From the college, proceed

A country house in Accomac, Virginia

along MD 12 to Snow Hill and then on VA 679 to Wattsville, Virginia, and the Chincoteague cutoff. On the second day, return to Wattsville and continue on VA 679 to Modest Town. From Modest Town take VA 187 and cross US 13 for Bloxom, Virginia. At Bloxom, follow VA 316 to Greenbush. From Greenbush take VA 764 to Accomac. From Accomac take Wachapreague Road/VA 605. Outside of Wachapreague, on the third day, take VA 600, which goes to Cheriton and Cape Charles.

This is strictly a one-way trip. Once you arrive at Cape Charles, you should plan on being picked up by van or car if you wish to return to Salisbury. Should you wish to continue south, you will have to take a bus with your bicycle through the Chesapeake Bay Bridge-Tunnel. (No cyclists are permitted on the bridge-tunnel.) You can catch an intercity bus traveling north or south at Paul's Restaurant in the village of Cheriton, Virginia.

Directions for the Ride

Day One: Salisbury to Chincoteague

0.0   College and Camden Avenues at Salisbury State College. Proceed east on College Avenue across US 13 and pass the Dresser-Wayne Pump Company on your right.

1.4   Turn right on MD 12/Snow Hill Road.

7.3   Worcester County line. Once you cross the county line the road gets wider.

13.9   Iron Furnace Road.

SIDE TRIP: If you wish, turn right here for a 4-mile diversion to the historic Nassawango Iron Furnace (see Tour 22).

17.5   Enter Snow Hill (see Tour 23).

17.9   Cross the Pocomoke River.

If you are looking for a few hours of lazy canoeing on the river or exploring the great Pocomoke Swamp, you can hire equipment as well as a guide at the Pocomoke River Canoe Company, which has headquarters at the bridge. (Open on weekends in the fall and spring, daily from Memorial Day to Labor Day; 410-632-3971.)

18.1   Turn right at the traffic light onto Market Street.

18.2   Turn left on Church Street/MD 12 to Girdletree and Stockton.

19.7   At the intersection and stop sign at US 113, cross US 113 and continue on MD 12.

24.0   Enter Girdletree.

There is a good country store here for cold drinks and snacks.

27.0   Enter Stockton.

27.5   In Stockton pass Fleming's Grocery Store at the crossroads of MD 366 and MD 12. Continue south on MD 12.

30.9   At the Virginia state line, MD 12 becomes VA 679. Continue on VA 679 south.

34.7   Horntown, Virginia.

38.9 *At the intersection of VA 679 and VA 175 turn left onto VA 175 for Chincoteague Island.*

Stop at Coffin's Market for cold drinks and excellent homemade sandwiches.

42.3 *NASA visitors center.*

The Wallops Island Facility, as it is known locally, was involved in American space research and rocketry in the 1950s, long before space exploration was news. NASA does important weather and satellite research here. The visitors center is open Thursday through Monday.

As you cross the VA 175 causeway to Chincoteague, proceed with the utmost caution. Summer traffic is heavy, and the two-lane road has no shoulder for cyclists.

47.7 *Main Street, Chincoteague.*

See Tour 24 for information on Chincoteague and Assateague.

Day Two: Chincoteague to Wachapreague

55.4 *Backtrack from Chincoteague Island to the intersection of VA 175 and VA 679. Turn left on VA 679, heading south.*

57.8 *Atlantic.*

Not as sleepy as it looks, the village of Atlantic has several stores and an excellent pharmacy located nearby on US 13.

65.8 *Enter Modest Town.*

The village's name says it all.

66.5 *Leave Modest Town passing the large Modest Town Baptist Church on your right. Turn right on VA 187.*

67.6 *Cross US 13 at Nelsonia and continue on VA 187 to Bloxom.*

69.2 *Enter Bloxom.*

You have entered the Deep South of Virginia's Eastern Shore. You'll see some depressing poverty on the outskirts of town. Bloxom is a slow-moving country town whose ways are not always fathomable to outsiders. With thousands of acres in the area planted in tomatoes and other truck crops, Bloxom is an important migrant labor center so you may hear some Spanish spoken. Stop at the local coffee shop at the corner of VA 187 and VA 316. Virginia shore people are friendly and curious about long-distance cyclists.

69.8 *Turn left on VA 316, which runs due south parallel to the Eastern Shore Railroad tracks.*

73.0 *Enter Parksley.*

This Victorian gem is a flourishing little town with clean streets and well-kept homes.

76.9 *At Greenbush, turn left on VA 764 for Accomac.*

78.1 *Cross US 13 and enter Accomac, the county seat of Accomack County.*

The Shore Stop convenience market at this intersection is the only place in Accomac to buy a sandwich, drink, or supplies. The local restaurant and store in town was purchased by county lawyers and turned into offices.

Northampton County Court House in Eastville, Virginia

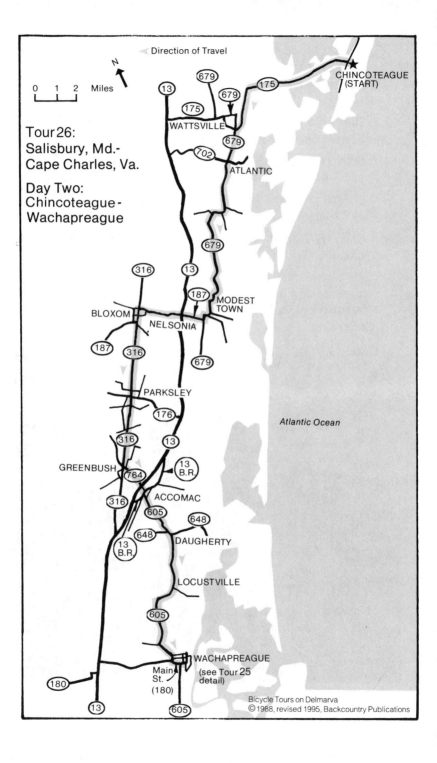

Direction of Travel

N

0 1 2 Miles

Tour 26:
Salisbury, Md.-
Cape Charles, Va.

Day Two:
Chincoteague-
Wachapreague

CHINCOTEAGUE
(START)

175

679

679

679

175

WATTSVILLE

13

679

702

ATLANTIC

679

13

187

MODEST
TOWN

316

BLOXOM

NELSONIA

187

316

679

PARKSLEY

176

Atlantic Ocean

316

13

GREENBUSH

764

13
B.R.

316

ACCOMAC

605

648

13
B.R.

648

DAUGHERTY

LOCUSTVILLE

605

180

13

WACHAPREAGUE
(see Tour 25
detail)

Main
St.
(180)

605

Bicycle Tours on Delmarva
©1988, revised 1995, Backcountry Publications

78.6 Accomac Debtors Prison is on your left.

This building was originally the 18th-century residence of both debtors and the county jailer.

SIDE TRIP: For a brief diversion, proceed straight ahead past the courthouse and across US Business Route 13. The mansion of antebellum governor Henry A. Wise will be on your right. At the memorial to Reverend Francis Makemie, the founder of Presbyterianism on the Eastern Shore in the 17th century, turn left onto a shady lane.

Many of the old Colonial homes of Accomac have been lovingly restored, and Accomac still appears much like an English country village.

Turn left on US Business Route 13 to resume your mileage count from the courthouse.

78.8 Turn left on VA 605/Wachapreague Road.

Note the splendid multichimney house on your left.

80.7 Village of Daugherty.

83.2 Enter Locustville.

When I last rode through here, this hamlet had a sign that boasted Locustville's population of 11. The Methodist church is on your right. The old Locustville Academy (1859) on your left is worth a look as well.

87.8 Turn left at the stop sign onto VA 180 for Wachapreague.

88.3 Enter Wachapreague and proceed down Main Street.

Wachapreague is the fishing capital of Virginia's Eastern Shore. Its docks are full of charter fishing boats and the flounder fishing here in the summer is the best around. The boats go out early in the morning, and at 5 AM the town is abuzz with activity. At the marina restaurant you can eat well on a budget and swap fish stories with the locals. At the Wachapreague Motel you can rent an outboard motorboat for the day and explore Parramore and Cedar Islands, the barrier island haunts of the famous 16th-century pirate, Blackbeard. Later in the day, sit in the Island House Restaurant and watch the boats come in.

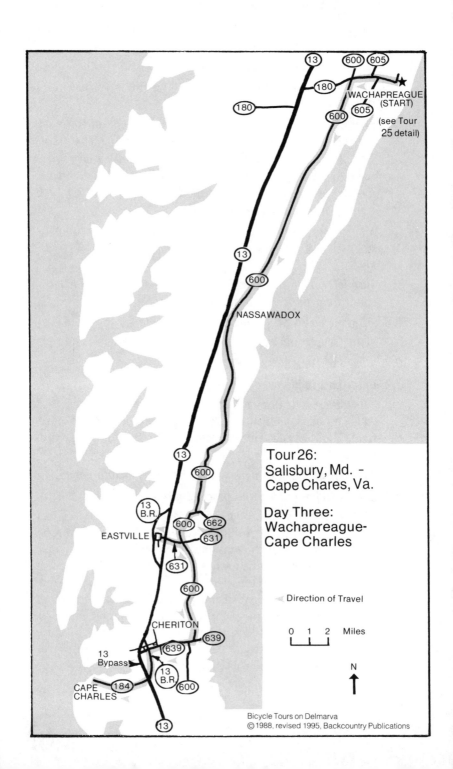

13

600 605

180

WACHAPREAGUE
(START)

(see Tour
25 detail)

180

600 605

13

600

NASSAWADOX

13

600

13
B.R.

600 662

EASTVILLE

631

631

600

CHERITON

639 639

13
Bypass

13
B.R.

CAPE 184
CHARLES

600

13

Tour 26:
Salisbury, Md. -
Cape Chares, Va.

Day Three:
Wachapreague-
Cape Charles

◁ Direction of Travel

0   1   2   Miles

N

↑

Bicycle Tours on Delmarva
© 1988, revised 1995, Backcountry Publications

Day Three: Wachapreague to Cape Charles

88.7 *Leave Wachapreague on VA 180.*

91.6 *Turn left and head south on VA 600. VA 600 parallels US 13 south.*

This farm road to Nassawadox and Cheriton has no country stores or service stations.

115.1 *SIDE TRIP: At the intersection of VA 600 and VA 631, you can take a 1.3-mile diversion on VA 631 to Eastville.*

Eastville is the seat of Northampton County. Here you can visit the oldest courthouse in Virginia still in use. Close by are the old one-room antebellum buildings still used as offices by Northampton County lawyers. Eastville is the smallest county seat on the Eastern Shore and has a population of 238.

Northampton County was one of the first eight shires created in Virginia in 1634 and was originally called Accomac. In 1643 the Virginia Eastern Shore was divided into two political units—Accomack County to the north and Northampton to the south. Northampton County played an important part in maintaining the first permanent English settlement at Jamestown by providing salt and meat to the settlement during its early existence. The old courthouse dates from 1730 and has the oldest court records in America. Have lunch in the historic Eastville Inn. Return to VA 600 at the point of diversion, turn right, and head south, resuming your mileage count.

119.6 *At the intersection of VA 600 and VA 639 turn right on VA 639 for Cheriton.*

121.0 *Enter Cheriton.*

This flourishing agribusiness center has an intercity bus stop at Paul's Restaurant on US Business Route 13.

121.9 *In Cheriton, turn left on US Business Route 13 and proceed south out of town.*

122.8 *Cross US 13 and take VA 184 to Cape Charles.*

124.6 *Enter Cape Charles and continue straight ahead on Randolph Avenue to the bay.*

125.0 Cape Charles Beach, gazebo, and promenade.

Cape Charles was established in 1884 when the New York, Philadelphia, and Norfolk Railroad extended its service from Philadelphia to Norfolk. Cape Charles flourished as a rail station and passenger-ferry port and became the largest town in Northampton County. The opening of the Chesapeake Bay Bridge-Tunnel in 1965 put an end to Cape Charles's ferry industry, and today the town is a bit down at the heels. The town beach and promenade are still lovely though. From here you have the rare opportunity in the East to see the sun set over water. Congratulations on the end of your century!

Bicycle Repair Services

Salisbury Schwinn Cyclery (410-546-4747), 1404 S. Salisbury Blvd., Salisbury, MD.

The Bikesmith (410-749-2453), 1503 N. Salisbury Blvd., Salisbury, MD.

Lodging

Birchwood Motel (804-336-6133) 3650 Main St., Chincoteague, VA 23336.

Rittenhouse Motor Lodge (804-331-2768), Box 288 (0.5 mile south of the US 13–Cape Charles interchange), Cape Charles, VA 23310.

Temple Hill Motel (410-742-3284), 1510 S. Salisbury Blvd. (0.5 mile south of Salisbury State College), Salisbury, MD 21801.

Wachapreague Motel (804-787-2105), PO Box 380, Main St., Wachapreague, VA 23480.

27
Kent Narrows–Ocean City, Maryland

Distance: 110 miles
Time and distance planning: 2 days. Kent Narrows to Salisbury: 73
   miles; Salisbury to Ocean City: 37 miles
Terrain: Rolling farmland
Location: Queen Anne's, Caroline, Dorchester, Wicomico, and Worcester
   Counties, Maryland
Special features: Kent Narrows, Wye Mills, Wye Oak, Martinak State
   Park, Salisbury, Berlin, Ocean City

This tour has been designed specifically to get the cyclist to the beach at
Ocean City without fighting summer and holiday traffic all the way from
Kent Island. It is not the most direct route, but it is certainly the safest
and most scenic. As there are few accommodations along this route, I
suggest that you attempt to cycle to Salisbury in one day.

On the Kent Narrows–Salisbury leg of your journey, you will cross
miles of open countryside, and the lack of shaded roads in the summer
makes for a sweltering ride. Make provisions for hot weather cycling.
When we took this route, my son Stewart and I left Kent Narrows at dawn
in order to take advantage of a cool July morning. In the afternoon, however, we were forced by the heat to take frequent stops for rest and water.

From Salisbury to Ocean City, the countryside is more varied and
more shaded. The country stores of Powellville are worth a visit. Berlin
is full of country bustle, and Ocean City froths with its mixture of neon,
Coney Island, condominium glitz, and tourist hustle.

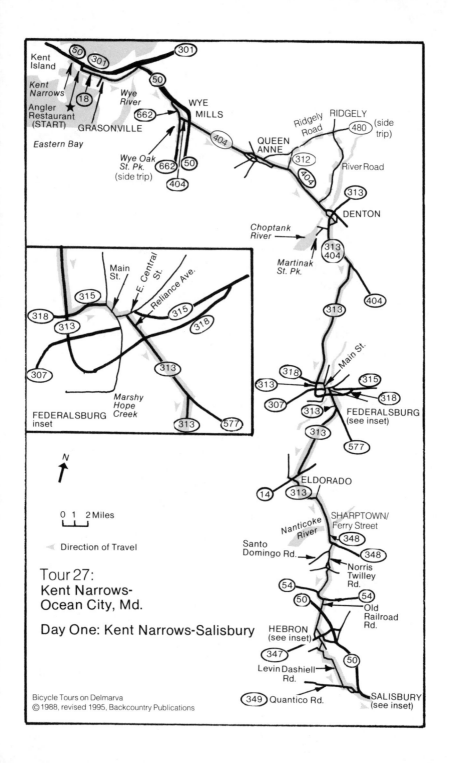

Directions for the Ride

0.0 *This tour begins at Kent Narrows on MD 18 at the parking lot of the Angler Restaurant. To get to the restaurant and starting point, take US 50 East by car from Annapolis and go to the end of Kent Island. Take the first right after the Kent Narrows drawbridge. At the intersection, turn right on MD 18 and proceed to the restaurant.*

MD 18 allows you to avoid the hectic traffic of US 50 and to experience the more relaxed atmosphere of marinas and seafood houses. In the morning at Kent Narrows you can watch elegant yachts and fishing vessels waiting for the bridge to rise so they can proceed outward to Eastern Bay and the pleasant waters of the Wye River.

Mount your bike at the Angler Restaurant and head east on MD 18.

1.2 *Enter the village of Grasonville.*

Here there are "juntique" shops and general stores for you to explore. Grasonville is rapidly entering the suburban orbit of Annapolis, and the traffic on MD 18 can be busy at times.

5.3 *At the junction with US 50, turn right onto US 50.*

Unfortunately, a small stretch of biking on this four-lane highway can't be avoided. Proceed with caution.

9.7 *Exit US 50 and turn right onto MD 662. This relatively deserted stretch of country highway will take you to Wye Mills.*

11.1 *Enter Wye Mills.*

A gristmill has stood on this site since the early 18th century. Flour ground here was shipped to General Washington's troops during the American Revolution. Though Wye Mills appears to be a sleepy village, it boasts a summer playhouse, producing musicals and serious drama, and a community college, Chesapeake College.

SIDE TRIP: Continue 1.2 miles on MD 662 and you will come to Wye Oak, the most famous tree in Maryland.

Believed to be over 400 years old, Wye Oak is 104 feet high and has a trunk 32 feet in circumference. Both the tree and an acre and

The Lifesaving Museum in Ocean City, Maryland

a half of land have been acquired by the state as a park. The best way to photograph Wye Oak and its nearby Colonial house is from the parking lot of the feed mill directly across the road from the tree.

The nearby Old Wye Church is an elegant 18th-century Episcopal chapel that has been completely restored. For a taste of local history, try Chesapeake beaten biscuits, sold next door at Orell's Bakery. Made from the old colonial recipe, the beaten biscuit was a staple during lean times and transatlantic voyages. It does not have a shelf life; it has a half life.

11.1 *From Wye Oak backtrack to MD 404 in the village of Wye Mills and go right on MD 404 East.*

12.2 *At the intersection of MD 404 and US 50, cross US 50 and proceed east on MD 404.*

"The 404" is a favorite with many bikers because it is a quick way to get to the beaches of southern Delaware. Once the 404 enters Delaware, it becomes an exceedingly unsafe road. I do not recommend it because the Delaware section of the 404 is clogged with summer traffic, has little or no shoulder for cyclists, and is poorly maintained by the state. I believe that the 404 is safe only as far as the cutoff at MD 313 to Federalsburg.

SIDE TRIP: If you have time, you can take an interesting side trip that will lead you through Ridgely and into Denton on an alternative route. Watch for a sign for MD 312. Turn left and proceed 1.4 miles to Ridgely Road. Turn right, and 1 mile more will take you into Ridgely.

Founded in 1867, Ridgely was supposed to be the first planned city on the Eastern Shore as an entrepôt of the Maryland and Delaware Railroad. Although the city never got off the drawing board, Ridgely survives as a quaint village. Its broad main street and false-front architecture make it resemble the stage set of a western town. (Two comfortable bed & breakfast inns in Ridgely are listed at the end of this chapter.)

From Ridgely, it is a 4-mile run down to Denton. Turn right on River Road. In 1 mile you'll reach MD 404 and the entrance to Denton.

24.2 *Continuing on MD 404 East, exit at Denton for downtown Denton. The road briefly becomes four lanes at the approach of the Choptank River Bridge. Go straight across the bridge on MD 404.*

25.4 *Enter Denton.*

The seat of Caroline County, Denton is the kind of Eastern Shore town that still thrills to firemen's parades, summer band concerts, and Fourth of July celebrations.

25.7 *The Denton Court House.*

The courthouse sits dreamily in the middle of a shaded lawn, and old-timers sit on park benches and watch traffic go by. Denton was once a major tomato-cannery center and steamboat landing. In the summer, take time to savor the fresh cantaloupes and vegetables sold locally at roadside stands.

25.8 *Turn left at the stop sign onto Franklin Street/MD 404. In Denton, MD 404 is one-way in each direction.*

27.7 Martinak State Park.

The park sits on the upper reaches of the Choptank River. This is a good place to take a picnic lunch and visit a log cabin museum of Native American artifacts.

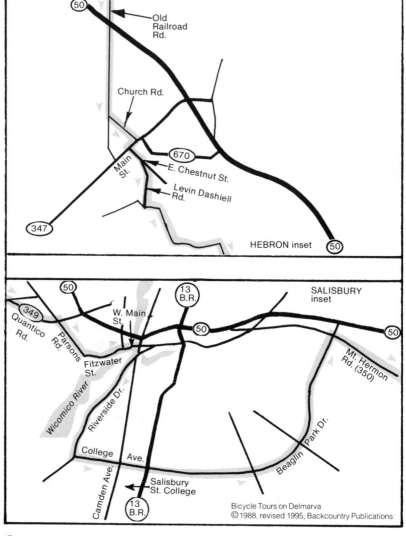

Bicycle Tours on Delmarva
© 1988, revised 1995, Backcountry Publications

31.2 Turn right on MD 313 and head south to Federalsburg.

41.3 For such a small town, the traffic pattern of Federalsburg can be confusing. You can bypass Federalsburg by swinging around the town on MD 313. Or you can turn left and enter the town at the traffic light on MD 315.

Federalsburg is larger than one would expect for such a rural area. The streets and shops have a 1950s quality to them. Most people work in local canneries, food processing plants, or in the textile mills of the DuPont Corporation in nearby Seaford, Delaware.

42.1 In Federalsburg, turn right on Bloomingdale Avenue, which becomes Main Street.

42.4 Turn left on East Central Street.

42.6 Turn right on Reliance Avenue. This will be the first right turn after crossing the bridge across Marshy Hope Creek.

43.1 At the traffic light and intersection of MD 318 and MD 313, continue on MD 313 South.

44.3 Keep right on MD 313 and enter Dorchester County.

51.2 Enter Eldorado. Keep left on MD 313.

The name of this hamlet is more romantic than its appearance.

56.5 Cross the Nanticoke River on a new bridge. At the end of the bridge, turn right and enter Sharptown.

Until World War II, Sharptown was a booming agricultural village and ship construction center. While time has passed it by, it still has a pickle factory, a country-and-western bar, and residents who think their village is the center of the universe. The local bar is friendly and serves ketchup-flavored potato chips. The locals are curious and friendly and love to talk about crabbing and fishing. In the summer you can smell crabs being steamed with Old Bay Seasoning on village stoves.

56.7 Turn left on Ferry Street.

57.0 At the blinker light, turn left on MD 348.

58.2 Turn right onto Santo Domingo Road.

Interestingly, many refugee French planters from Haiti settled in Maryland after the black nationalist slave revolt led by Toussaint

Louverture in the 1790s. The old name for Haiti, Santo Domingo, is now part of the Maryland landscape.

58.8 *Turn left onto Norris Twilley Road. Caution: Norris Twilley is unpaved but navigable for 2 miles.*

62.6 *Reach the end of Norris Twilley Road. At the stop sign turn left onto MD 54.*

63.3 *Turn right onto Old Railroad Road, heading south.*

64.1 *Cross US 50 and continue south.*

65.7 *Turn left onto Church Road and proceed to Hebron.*

66.2 *Enter Hebron.*

An old railroad village dating from the 1890s, Hebron has quiet back streets and roads. The town has a large grocery store and a restaurant for weary and hungry cyclists.

66.3 *Turn right on Main Street. Go past the IGA Supermarket on your right.*

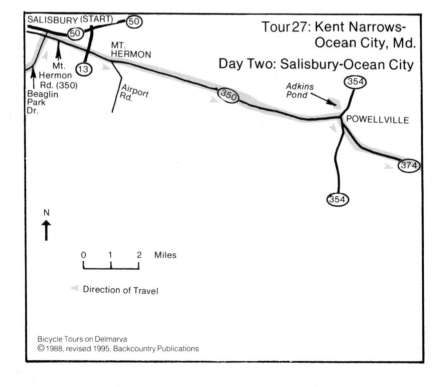

Tour 27: Kent Narrows–Ocean City, Md.

Day Two: Salisbury–Ocean City

Bicycle Tours on Delmarva
© 1988, revised 1995, Backcountry Publications

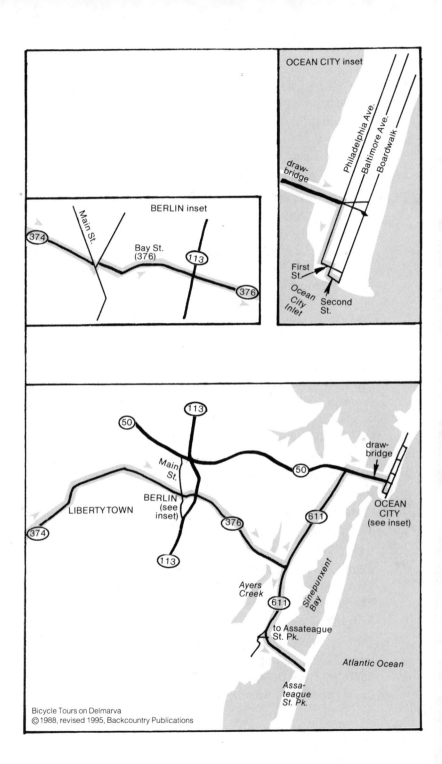

OCEAN CITY inset

Philadelphia Ave.
Baltimore Ave.
Boardwalk

draw-bridge

First St.
Second St.

Ocean City Inlet

BERLIN inset

Main St.

Bay St. (376)

374

113

376

113

50

Main St.

LIBERTYTOWN

BERLIN (see inset)

50

draw-bridge

OCEAN CITY (see inset)

374

376

611

113

Ayers Creek

Sinepuxent Bay

611

to Assateague St. Pk.

Atlantic Ocean

Assa-teague St. Pk.

66.5 *Turn left on East Chestnut Street at the Hebron carnival grounds.*

Like many towns here on the Eastern Shore, the volunteer fire department of Hebron hosts a carnival each year to raise money to buy equipment.

66.7 *Turn right onto Levin Dashiell Road.*

71.5 *Reach the end of Levin Dashiell Road. At the stop sign turn left onto Quantico Road/MD 349. Enter Salisbury.*

Salisbury is the largest town on the Eastern Shore, with a metropolitan population in excess of 60,000. It has been a major port in the region since the 1790s and ranks after Baltimore and Crisfield for ship-freight tonnage in the state. Recently economic growth, particularly in the service sector, has transformed Salisbury from a farming center of feed mills and fertilizer plants into an important medical, legal, and food-processing center. Salisbury is the home of Perdue Chicken Inc. and the capital of the entire Delmarva broiler chicken industry. Its growth, however, has not detracted from its being a very livable urban center, and cyclists can enjoy the parks and city zoo. Even more important, cyclists can move in and out of Salisbury with little difficulty, as traffic even in rush hour has yet to become bothersome.

72.5 *Turn right on Parsons Road and pass Prestige Autos on your right. As you approach the crest of a hill you will overlook a shipyard.*

73.0 *Parsons Road becomes Fitzwater Street then West Main Street.*

The flourishing shipyard stands in stark contrast to the substandard neighborhood.

73.5 *Continue on West Main and cross the small steel drawbridge. Turn right at the traffic light. Bear right on Riverside Drive. The Wicomico River will be on your right. Continue on Riverside Drive.*

74.6 *Turn left on College Avenue and continue straight through the intersection and traffic light of Camden and College Avenues. Salisbury State College will be on your right. Cross US 13, continuing on College Avenue, which becomes Beaglin Park Drive.*

Inlet at Ocean City, Maryland (*photo by Orlando V. Wootten*)

78.0 *Turn right on Mt. Hermon Road/MD 350.*

80.4 *Pass through the hamlet of Mt. Hermon. At the intersection with Airport Road (nearby is Salisbury's airport, with passenger service to Baltimore and Washington) where you find Ward's Cash Market, continue on MD 350 through the Wicomico County Nature Preserve.*

Stop along the way to enjoy the cool shade and the wildfowl life of the preserve.

88.4 *Enter Powellville.*

Boasting two general stores, Powellville is an excellent resting place. The stores serve coffee and sandwiches. Cycle over to the nearby dam and relax at Adkins Pond for awhile.

89.0 *At the intersection of MD 350 and MD 354, turn right on MD 354.*

The countryside is very pretty through here. Enjoy the patches of shade on the road.

89.4 *Turn left on MD 374. If you miss this turn for Ocean City, you will end up in Snow Hill.*

94.1 *Pass through the hamlet of Libertytown.*

98.7 *Enter Berlin, a shady, pleasant town.*

Berlin's winding streets contain interesting Colonial and Victorian homes, and the business section is compact and prosperous.

99.5 *Take care not to miss the Bay Street turn. At Farlow's Pharmacy on Main Street, make a sharp right turn, then left at the Peninsula Bank. Bear right on Bay Street/MD 376.*

99.9 *There is a traffic light at the intersection of US 113 and MD 376. Continue on MD 376.*

103.4 *Ayers Creek Bridge.*

You have a lovely waterfront vista. Often you will see people on the bridge fishing and catching crabs.

104.1 *At the junction of MD 376 and MD 611 you have two options.*

SIDE TRIP: You can turn right and follow MD 611 to Assateague State Park and its beaches. After 3 miles you will come to a large bridge that will take you across Sinepuxent Bay to Assateague Island.

The island is a great sandbar whose permanent residents are waterfowl and wild ponies that have been there since Spanish galleons wrecked off the coast in the 16th century. The area is still wild and is very popular with backpackers, sport anglers, and campers. Although it is fun to walk along the dunes and swim at the beach at Assateague, bear in mind that there is no shade on the island and the sandy roads are difficult to navigate on a bicycle. Still, you have 35 miles of undeveloped beach to stroll along to search for sand dollars and other interesting shells.

If you choose the other option, turn left and proceed to Ocean City.

Caution: MD 611 is busy in summer, especially where it passes Ocean City's airport.

108.1 *At the intersection of MD 611 and US 50, turn right onto US 50. Cross the drawbridge into Ocean City.*

Because of the resort traffic on the bridge, use the sidewalk. The bridge sidewalk is fenced off to protect walkers and anglers.

110.0 After the bridge, turn right on Philadelphia Avenue and proceed to the Ocean City inlet and the Ocean City Lifesaving Museum. You will now be at the water's edge on First Street.

This is a pretty part of the resort, and the beach is wide. Despite the strong currents at the inlet, there is plenty of boat traffic and always a throng of people fishing from a large stone jetty.

A few comments about Ocean City will suffice: Some will see Ocean City as a noisy seaside honky-tonk run amuck with neon-covered commercial development. Others see a popular family resort with boardwalk promenades, food stands, and amusements for children. I prefer the old part of Ocean City near the inlet to the high-rise Gold Coast to the north.

Ocean City has been a resort since 1872. With the coming of the railroad and the construction of a bridge to the mainland, Ocean City boomed, and it has never stopped booming. The town has always been the home of slick promoters and real estate speculators. Note that Ocean City does have a crime problem in the summer, mostly with petty theft, so keep an eye on your bicycle.

Despite my personal cynicism about the place, I have enjoyed my visits to Ocean City. Cycling on the boardwalk provides a glorious ride at dawn when the surf is breaking. In season, cycling is permitted on the boardwalk until 10 AM. I have also enjoyed the clean beaches, which are well patrolled by excellent lifeguards. And, if you are a youthful, blithe spirit, nothing beats the social action of Ocean City.

Bicycle repair service

Continental Cycles (410-524-1313), 7203 Coastal Hwy., Ocean City, MD.

Attractions

Chesapeake Railroad (410-482-2330), Ridgely, MD. This 10-mile excursion train, featuring a 1912 Pullman parlor car, runs from Ridgely Memorial Park to Queen Anne on weekends May through October.

Old Denton Schoolhouse (410-479-3614), Franklin and Second Sts., Denton, MD. Open by request.

Wicomico Heritage Center (410-543-0651), Handy Plantation and Pemberton Historical Park, Salisbury, MD. Headquarters of the Wicomico Historical Society. Delightful park and grounds of an 18th-century tidewater plantation. See Tour 16.

Lodging

Duning Studio Bed and Breakfast (410-634-2491), 24451 Burn Mill Dr., Ridgely, MD 21660. 3 rooms, private baths.

Econo Lodge (410-524-5634), 102 60th St., Ocean City, MD 21842.

Holland House Bed and Breakfast (410-641-1956), 5 Bay St., Berlin, MD 21811. 5 rooms, private baths.

Sophie Kerr House (410-479-3421), Route 3, Box 7-B, Denton, MD 21629.

Taylor House Bed and Breakfast (410-289-1177), 1101 Baltimore Ave., Ocean City, MD 21842. 4 rooms, private baths.

Temple Hill Motel (410-742-3284), 1510 S. Salisbury Blvd., Salisbury, MD 21801.

Campground

There is a public campground at Assateague State Park. For further information contact Assateague National Seashore (410-641-1441), Route 2, Box 294, Berlin, MD 21811. (If you have never camped out on an open beach before, prepare for the sand flies!)

Appendix 1

General Information on Travel and Tourism

Maryland's Eastern Shore

Cecil County, Office of Economic Development (410-398-0200, ext. 144), County Office Building, Room 300, Elkton, MD 21921.

Kent County Chamber of Commerce (410-778-0416), PO Box 146, 118 N. Cross St., Chestertown, MD 21620.

Talbot County Chamber of Commerce (410-822-4606), PO Box 1366, Easton, MD 21601.

Dorchester County Tourism (410-228-3234), PO Box 307, Cambridge, MD 21613.

Somerset County Bureau of Tourism (410-651-2968), PO Box 243, Princess Anne, MD 21853.

Ocean City Visitors Bureau (410-289-8181), Box 116 (OTD), Ocean City, MD 21842.

Southern Delaware

Lewes Chamber of Commerce (302-645-8073), PO Box 1, Lewes, DE 19958.

New Castle Court House (302-323-4453), Delaware St., New Castle, DE 19720.

223

Rehoboth Beach Chamber of Commerce (1-800-441-1329), PO Box 216, Rehoboth Beach, DE 19971.

Eastern Shore of Virginia

Chincoteague Chamber of Commerce (804-336-6161), PO Box 258, Chincoteague, VA 23336.

New Jersey

Cape May Chamber of Commerce (609-465-7181), Cape May Court House, PO Box 74, Cape May, NJ 08210.

Appendix 2

Inns and Bed & Breakfast Accommodations

Bed & breakfast accommodations are not to be confused with private inns or guest houses. Usually these B&Bs are in private homes. The great advantage of these accommodations is a good price, congenial surroundings, and hosts who care about their guests. Should you require a B&B during one of your cycle trips in the Chesapeake, the following agencies can arrange a booking for you.

Maryland

The Traveler in Maryland (410-269-6232), 33 West St., Annapolis, MD 21401.

Amanda's Reservation Service (410-225-0001), 1428 Park Ave., Baltimore MD 21217.

Virginia

Bed and Breakfast of Tidewater Virginia (804-627-1983), Box 3343, Norfolk, VA 23514.

Delaware

Bed and Breakfast of Delaware (302-479-9500), 1804 Breen La., Wilmington, DE 19810.

The following is a list of inns that welcome cyclists and participate in inn-to-inn bicycle-touring packages.

Delaware

Spring Garden Bed and Breakfast (302-875-7015), Rt. 1, Box 283A, Delaware Ave. Extended, Laurel, DE 19956.

The Towers (302-422-3814), 101 NW Front St., Milford, DE 19963.

The Banking House (302-422-5708), 112 NW Front St., Milford, DE 19963.

Ganvier-Black House B&B (302-328-1339), 17 The Strand, New Castle, DE 19720.

Maryland

Nanticoke Manor House (410-376-3530), Church and Water Sts., Vienna, MD 21869.

Holland House (410-641-1956), 5 Bay St., Berlin, MD 21811.

The Tavern House (410-376-3347), 111 Water St., Box 98, Vienna, MD 21869.

The Bishop's House Bed and Breakfast (410-820-7290), PO Box 2217, 214 Goldsborough St., Easton, MD 21601.

Hayman House circa 1898 (410-651-2753), 117 Prince William St., Princess Anne, MD 21853.

Inn at the Canal (410-885-5995), 104 Bohemia Ave., Chesapeake City, MD 21915.

Commodore's Cottage (410-228-6938), 215 Glenburn Ave., Cambridge, MD 21613.

Two Swan Inn (410-745-2929), Foot Carpenter St., PO Box 727, St. Michaels, MD 21663.

John S. McDaniel House (410-822-3704), 14 N. Aurora St., Easton, MD 21601.

Brampton Bed & Breakfast (410-778-1832), RR 2, Box 107, Chestertown, MD 21620.

Lantern Inn (410-348-5809), 115 Ericsson Ave., PO Box 29, Betterton, MD 21610.

For more information about the packages these inns provide, contact Gwen North, Spring Garden Bed and Breakfast (302-875-7015), DE 1, Box 283A, Delaware Ave. Extended, Laurel, DE 19956.

Appendix 3

Bicycle Camping in Chesapeake Bay Country

Many of you will be cycling in the Chesapeake during good weather in either spring or summer. Camping offers an inexpensive and very enjoyable alternative to staying in costly inns or motels. Because of weight limitations, keep your gear to the basics: small two-person tent, sleeping bag, ground cloth, and eating utensils.

These campgrounds are listed in accordance with the tours that you may be taking on the Eastern Shore.

Tour 2, Tour 3, Tour 4

Duck Neck Campground (410-778-3070), RD 1, Box 262, Chestertown, MD 21620.

Tour 5, Tour 6, Tour 7

Cape Henlopen State Park (302-875-7543), Lewes, DE 19958.

Tour 14, Tour 27

Assateague National Seashore (410-641-1441), Route 2, Box 294, Berlin, MD 21811.

Tour 16, Tour 17, Tour 18

Princess Anne Campground (410-651-1520), Box 427, Princess Anne, MD 21853.

Tour 20, Tour 21

Janes Island State Park (410-968-1565), Crisfield, MD 21817.

Tour 24, Tour 26

Tom's Cove Camp Ground (804-336-6498), PO Box 122, Chincoteague, VA 23336.

Let Backcountry Guides Take You There

Our experienced backcountry authors will lead you to the finest trails, parks, and back roads in the following areas:

50 Hikes Series

50 Hikes in the Adirondacks
50 Hikes in Connecticut
50 Hikes in the Maine Mountains
50 Hikes in Southern and Coastal Maine
50 Hikes in Massachusetts
50 Hikes in Michigan
50 Hikes in the White Mountains
50 More Hikes in New Hampshire
50 Hikes in New Jersey
50 Hikes in the Hudson Valley
50 Hikes in Central New York
50 Hikes in Western New York
50 Hikes in the Mountains of North Carolina
50 Hikes in Ohio
50 Hikes in Eastern Pennsylvania
50 Hikes in Central Pennsylvania
50 Hikes in Western Pennsylvania
50 Hikes in Vermont
50 Hikes in Northern Virginia

Walks and Rambles Series

Walks and Rambles on Cape Cod and the
   Islands
Walks and Rambles on the Delmarva Peninsula
Walks and Rambles in the Western
   Hudson Valley
Walks and Rambles on Long Island
Walks and Rambles in Ohio's Western
   Reserve
Walks and Rambles in Rhode Island
More Walks and Rambles in Rhode Island
Walks and Rambles in and around St. Louis

25 Bicycle Tours Series

25 Bicycle Tours in the Adirondacks
25 Bicycle Tours on Cape Cod and the
   Islands
25 Bicycle Tours in Coastal Georgia and the
   Carolina Low Country
25 Bicycle Tours in Maine
25 Bicycle Tours in Maryland
25 Bicycle Tours in the Twin Cities and
   Southeastern Minnesota
30 Bicycle Tours in New Jersey
30 Bicycle Tours in the Finger Lakes Region
25 Bicycle Tours in the Hudson Valley
25 Bicycle Tours in Ohio's Western Reserve
25 Bicycle Tours in the Texas Hill Country
   and West Texas
25 Bicycle Tours in Vermont
25 Bicycle Tours in and around
   Washington, D.C.
30 Bicycle Tours in Wisconsin
25 Mountain Bike Tours in the Adirondacks
25 Mountain Bike Tours in the Hudson Valley
25 Mountain Bike Tours in Massachusetts
25 Mountain Bike Tours in New Jersey
25 Mountain Bike Tours in Vermont
Backroad Bicycling in Connecticut
The Mountain Biker's Guide to Ski Resorts

Bicycling America's National Parks Series

Bicycling America's National Parks: California
Bicycling America's National Parks: Utah &
   Colorado

We offer many more books on hiking, fly-fishing, travel, nature, and other subjects. Our books are available at bookstores and outdoor stores everywhere. For more information or a free catalog, please call 1-800-245-4151 or write to us at The Countryman Press, P.O. Box 748, Woodstock, Vermont 05091. You can find us on the Internet at http://www.countrymanpress.com.